Queer Returns

Queer Returns

*Essays on Multiculturalism,
Diaspora, and Black Studies*

Rinaldo Walcott

INSOMNIAC PRESS

Library and Archives Canada Cataloguing in Publication

Walcott, Rinaldo, 1965-, author
Queer returns : essays on multiculturalism, diaspora
and black studies / Rinaldo Walcott.

ISBN 978-1-55483-174-6 (paperback)

1. Queer theory. 2. Blacks--Race identity. 3. African diaspora.
4. Sexual minorities. 5. Multiculturalism. 6. Gays, Black. 7. Group
identity. 8. Geography--Psychological aspects. I. Title.

HQ76.25.W36 2016   306.76'608996   C2016-906833-1

The publisher gratefully acknowledges the support of the Canada
Council for the Arts and the Ontario Arts Council.

Printed and bound in Canada

Insomniac Press
520 Princess Avenue, London, Ontario, Canada, N6B 2B8
www.insomniacpress.com

Contents

Introduction:
Queer Returns
and Other Moments to Come

These essays span over a decade of returns. The returns are framed by my ongoing engagements and entanglements with cultural and political concerns routed through Black being, Black life, and its experiences. For more than twenty years, my scholarship has sought to bring blackness into a conversation demonstrating how Black people's contributions to global life, first in Canada and then beyond, might animate new ways of being in the world. The essays collected here continue that work. These essays also mark the ongoing maturity of a scholar attempting to figure out how to return to scenes of previous engagements in ways that demonstrate growth, change, and doubt. The dilemma of working across, within, and against the anti-Black formation of the university is central to the work collected here, even though not explicitly marked as such. In this way, these essays represent a continuing intellectual development that is far from achieved.

Queer Returns, then, returns to familiar themes in my body of work such as diaspora, multiculturalism, sexuality, nation, and citizenship. In each return I seek to ask a set of questions at a specific historical moment that aim to produce an account of our time in which a focus on Black lives and their expressivity might clarify what exactly is at stake for all of us. These essays center Black people, not because Black people are exceptional, but rather because I maintain the position that Black people are central to the larger and deeper fulfillment of what we call freedom. As our present time marks so clearly, the question of freedom and Black people is one that is in deep crisis. Freedom has been and remains a stubborn global impossibility for Black people everywhere. And yet the essays collected here hint at a number of ways in which Black people continue to apprehend and seize moments of freedom. In each case the seizure of freedom is interdicted and the process begins anew.

Questions of what it means to be human, of queerness, and of citizenship and nation return us to freedom, but most of all those questions when threaded through Black life remind us of freedom's elusive qualities. In the place of freedom we notice the structures that uphold status quo practices, and we are forced to notice that those status quo practices are often premised on ways of being that offer Black life and Black beings no place to achieve the ideals marked and claimed as freedom. In these essays, I engage debates on multiculturalism, reconciliation, LGBT identities and politics, diaspora, and other conceptual and identity politically driven narratives and debates; each essay suggests that what might be at stake is how we think about the problem at hand. Indeed, it is often the very question of thought that is at stake when blackness and Black people enter the central frame of the conversation.

Following from the above, Black Studies, as a multidisciplinary and interdisciplinary intellectual formation, has been the touchstone from which these essays find their voice and their mode of utterance and from which they emerge. The politically engaged demand of Black Studies that begins with the politics of thought as engaged in the project of and the struggle for freedom is what stands behind each essay. Black Studies in these essays is not only both breadth and range, but also a demand that knowledge means something beyond the institutional confines of the university. These essays are marked by an attempt to make use of the university as a site to engage both it and other institutions as fundamental sites for ongoing freedom struggles. The university then is merely a base from which a Black Studies engaged scholarship might launch an assault on multiple institutions complicit and actively engaged in the work of (Black) unfreedom. Black Studies in these essays is the ongoing incitement that the work of freedom is not yet over, that freedom is not yet achieved.

Significantly, most of these essays are influenced by the aftermath of the September 11, 2001 events in the USA. While not every essay explicitly addressed those events now singularized and globalized as "9/11," most of them have it as their backdrop because the aftermath of the event, now singular too, required that we rethink so much of what in the 1990s had seemed almost settled or on the way to being settled. Debates about nation, religion, citizenship, multiculturalism, diaspora, colonialism, sexuality, gender, and on and on have now all been caught up in the aftermath of 9/11 in a way that restages the most urgent questions of the mid-twentieth century, tackled in the 1960s and after. The restaging of these questions of liberation, which seemed on the way to being settled, has returned us to deeper conceptual questions and concerns about the global organization of all human life. One might argue that in a strange way the violence unleashed post-9/11 globally has forced us to think anew about what it means to be human.

In my view, it is what it means to be human that is ultimately at stake. The struggle over the category of the human marks these essays in indelible ways. Again, because Black people are often so firmly ejected from the current, partial definition of what it means to be human, when Black people are centered, other modes of being emerge. These essays grapple with those other modes of being to insist that new modes of being human are indeed possible. To argue for new modes of being human is not to suggest some easy notion of hope that rests in a renovation and reforming of the world as it presently is. Rather, the grappling with what it means to be human is a more radical call for an entire and total transformation of the globe as it presently is.

Queer Returns, finally, returns us to the scene of colonialism and its central practice of African enslavement and its afterlives as necessary and urgent, yet banal, elements of our everyday global formations. These essays do not seek to tell a coherent story of African and Indigenous colonization, enslavement, and dispossession, but rather to evoke the ways in which those processes are adaptable, irrational, and entirely framed through a logic of white supremacy that seeks to maintain a very specific global order.

Rinaldo Walcott
August 2016
Toronto

Chapter 1

Dramatic Instabilities: Diasporic Aesthetics As a Question for and about Nation

Introduction: Producing Dramatic Instabilities

Let's begin with a major claim. Black Canadian theatre is forged and performed within the context of a diasporic sensibility and/or consciousness. Thus, Black Canadian theatre sits somewhere between addressing its "nationally-local" contexts and engaging in a much wider context: that wider context is the basis of what constitutes its diasporic aesthetics. So let's make one further claim: Black Canadian theatre is centrally concerned with the piecing together of all the ways in which diasporic expressions of blackness can fashion a commentary on its nationally-local and global conditions. What I mean by this is that the form, the performance, the texture, the content, and the gesture of Black Canadian theatre engages its nationally-local context and beyond. In this essay I will probe a number of Black Canadian plays to demonstrate how the execution of those plays produces a diasporic sensibility and consciousness and thus a diasporic aesthetic, and how those plays represent a dramatic instability for nationally-local concerns by reaching beyond the nationally-local, as well as speaking specifically and directly to the nationally-local context in uncompromising fashion. The various moves or aesthetic practices that I attempt to map from these plays are what I call "dramatic instabilities." These dramatic instabilities are not negative consequences of the plays; rather, these instabilities are dramatic in their demands for a more ethical constitution of the nationally-local scene and condition for making a life that is Black and livable both national and international.

When the ethical is inserted into the conversation as a form of concern, some different manner of outcome might be expected. The philosopher of New World conditions, Sylvia Wynter, in the essay "Rethinking 'Aesthetics': Notes Towards a Deciphering Practice," offers a reading of the now classic 1972 Jamaican film *The Harder They Come*. In Wynter's reading of the film, she proposes what she calls a "deciphering practice." By a deciphering practice Wynter means to signal some rather important ways of reading and making sense of texts (broadly defined) so that we can move between and beyond the specifics of what she calls "ethno-criticism" and into a reconstituted universalism proffered from the vantage point of the subaltern or the dispossessed. Thus, for her "a deciphering turn seeks to decipher *what* the process of rhetorical mystification *does*. It seeks to identify not what texts and their signifying practices can be interpreted to *mean* but what they can be deciphered to do, and it also seeks to evaluate the 'illocutionary force' and procedures with which they do what they do."[1] Furthermore, Wynter posits that the question of taste is important to a deciphering practice because it challenges the Western middle-class cultural imaginary in an attempt to offer a counter-politics that seeks to produce a "global popular Imaginary whose referent telos is that of the well-being of the individual human subject and, therefore, of the species."[2] Thus, a deciphering practice is about attempting to engage in a political process that concerns itself with changing our present governing orders of rule for both individuals and the collective body politic.

The Instabilities of the Nationally-Local

Sylvia Wynter, in attempting to think the political inside the aesthetic, is not at all trying to reduce art to a crass notion of politics. Rather, Wynter attempts to argue and demonstrate that art always speaks for some kind of politics. I agree with such an analysis. In ahdri zhina mandiela's *dark diaspora... in dub*, the opening lines immediately reference or gesture to a wide expanse of Black diaspora interests. The lines move from the individual to the collective ("& this:one / of many / million / dark tales"); to a nod to the "dream deferred" in Langston Hughes' "Harlem" ("let out / blocked hopes"); to the dilemma of oral performativity and the written word ("these words are / for / ever / / more / just fossilled: / language"). This span of gesture in just the opening lines of the play is but one moment or instance of the invocation of a diasporic sensibility and/or consciousness. The play itself spans the Caribbean (Jamaica), African (Liberia), and the "white" Western world (Canada, Australia, London, etc.). The real and symbolic use of movement in the play is parallel to the forced and other forms of migration that Black diasporic people have undergone and continue to experience. The play itself is populated with all kinds of movement: migration to Canada, a poem called "blues bus," and various other forms of metaphoric and actual movement. This ongoing concern and reference to movement is, I believe, one of the central tenets of Black diasporic sensibilities and consciousnesses. And when these are etched into art, in this case a play, they become the basis of a diasporic aesthetics.

In the title poem from which the play takes its name, the culmination of the desires of the dark diaspora is exposed when the narrator chants "better mus come!" This chant is in part a counter-political act of the play whereby politics lives in its aesthetic demand for a different world, a more ethical world. Thus, it might be suggested that *dark diaspora … in dub* is intended to do something. "Better mus come" is the plea for what that something might signify or mean. A close reading of mandiela's play can produce a wealth of references to issues and concerns that one can broadly contextualize within a diasporic framework. But one of the central concerns of the play's overall aesthetic is to impact its nationally-local scene. It does so by a continued return and reference to the conditions of Black migration to Canada and the links between that migration and other Black people worldwide. A politics of identification transnationally is a signal of the Black diasporic aesthetic.

Similarly, Andrew Moodie's *Riot* offers a much more sustained concentration on the nationally-local as a way to impact and affect the national. So if mandiela begins in the wider diaspora and contracts to Canada, and then moves again, Moodie begins in the nationally-local, moves to the diasporic, and contracts to the nationally-local again. Each of these plays is interested in clarifying something about the nationally-local nature of Black experience and history in relation to the national and/or as an example of diasporic conditions. Moodie's play takes its inspiration from the Rodney King beating, and more specifically from the acquittal of the policemen responsible for it and the resulting riots in Los Angeles in 1992. *Riot* is, as well, a restaging of the 1992 riots on Yonge Street in Toronto that occurred in response to the acquittal of a policeman for shooting a Black man in Toronto. The ways in which the Yonge Street riots mirror the LA riots cannot be easily overlooked. While the Yonge Street riots were smaller and had less of a national and international impact than the LA riots, their nationally-local significance cannot be downplayed.

Using the Yonge Street riots as the backdrop of his play, Moodie set out to script a history and experience of Black Canadian-ness that would trouble previous definitions of blackness in Canada (at least on the stage). The characters of *Riot* are a multiethnic cast of Black players (Jamaican, Ugandan, Canadian). This particular representation of Canadian blackness sets into motion different kinds of attachments to the nation. Thus, what Canada means to each character is very different and is open for debate among the characters in the play, as it is among the audience. I have made two claims about *Riot* elsewhere: 1) that blackness must be understood as internally differentiated and as a set of competing histories; and 2) that the play elaborates our understanding of Canadian-ness. One way to read the characters of *Riot* is to see the cast as an ensemble of diasporic characters in Canada.[3] While all the characters are citizens of Canada, each has a different historical attachment to the nation, and each character brings a different sensibility to what the nation means to them. This difference in what the nation means destabilizes how it is that both the nation and blackness might be read. The destabilization lies in the difficult fact that neither nation nor blackness can be easily pinned down even though each is posited with a set of parameters that make them identifiable but not definable. The boundaries of nation are stretched to include more than it is assumed the nation can include. In such an instance, for example, Moodie's *Riot* elaborates the Canadian nation by recourse to positing a range of Black characters whose differences render any suggestion of a singular blackness or Black community impossible. And yet he is still able to produce forms of identification, which makes this multiethnic blackness identify with and act in solidarity with forms of African American blackness.

Moodie's *A Common Man's Guide to Loving Women* is similarly driven by the cross-border identification with the controversies, ramifications, and implications of Black manhood in the midst and aftermath of the OJ Simpson trials. *A Common Man's Guide* is in part an exploration of the ways in which particular representations of Black manhood circulate across North

America.[4] The play is also concerned with the historical and ongoing destabilizations of Black manhood. Without recourse to being didactic the play concerns itself with the historical constitution of Black manhood in a post-Columbus world. The most recent instance of the overwhelming troubles of Black manhood were spectacularized in the OJ Simpson trials, and the play makes use of this public collective memory to attempt to rescue some space for the complexities of Black manhood and, I would suggest, other (heterosexual) manhoods as well. In this way, the play does not just speak for blackness, but much like the ways in which *Riot* elaborates Canadian-ness, *A Common Man's Guide* forces us to confront the question of whether contemporary expressions of Black manhood can stand in for all of North American manhood and its present destabilization in the face of some important feminist gains that are remaking our patriarchal rules of governing.

A Common Man's Guide might be generously read as concerned with the destabilizations that contemporary feminism has wrought for all men about the context and practice of masculinity. In such a reading, the play addresses a particular set of questions and problematics about what might be a reconstituted masculinity in the face of a popular feminist consciousness. That the play launched this question through a discussion of Black manhood opens up the difficult terrain of whether subaltern experience and history can be the basis of and for a universalist understanding of human life. Thus, once again we see how a diasporic sensibility comes to engage an aesthetic inside which a politics of some sort lives. Once again transnational identification is evident. But to posit that the reviled, criminalized, and sometimes murdered manhood of Blackness might speak for all of manhood is to destabilize modernity and universality as some of us have come to know and understand those ideas. It is my argument that diasporic sensibilities are intimately engaged in processes of destabilization that are meant to produce a different view of the world and therefore a different aesthetic. Thus, I am suggesting that part of the aesthetics of Black Canadian theatre is a question of what might constitute a universal point of view from the vantage point of the subaltern.

Because the plays that I have discussed above (and those that I will discuss below) take their insight and sometimes inspiration from events, histories, moments, and other ephemera real and imagined from elsewhere, it is difficult to make sense of those plays without also having to think differently about the nation — in this case Canada. These plays destabilize the assumptions that produce the normative narrative of the nation as white, benevolent, and just. Instead, these plays find room for blackness and Black peoples, these plays posit a history of injustice and degradation, these plays offer forms of nationally-local resistance and international political identifications, and finally these plays refuse to accept that national contexts are the only meaningful contexts for justice, all the while holding the national context accountable, responsible, and ethically implicated. These plays rethink humanity and the universal from the vantage point of the dispossessed.

The Instabilities of Modernity, Universality, and Diaspora

Diasporic sensibilities are located in what we might characterize as a particular form of or insight into the universal. The idea of the universal is and remains one of the central tenets of the discourses of modernity. Because diasporic experiences might be characterized as the "B-side" of historical and contemporary discourses of globalization, diasporic experiences tend to reference and point directly to the ongoing traumas and injustices of the pre-modern, the modern, and the postmodern worlds. Thus, diasporic insights can provide us with a perspective on the universal from a non-dominant source. To do so, those who see themselves as outside the story of suffering and pain must find ways to identify with such stories so that the insights of those stories can become a site of solidarity and ethicality. As Paul Gilroy has pointed out, using the term "strategic universalism":

> Bolstered by the cautious, strategic universalism toward which the history of fascism inclines us, diverse stories of suffering can be recognized as belonging to anyone who dares to possess them and in good faith employ them as interpretative devices through which we may clarify the limits of our selves, the basis of our solidarities, and perhaps pronounce upon the value of our values. [5]

Diasporic experiences thus reference another kind

of universality; it is the universal position of the dispossessed from the fruits of modernity. These stories of suffering can offer us a new worldview for thinking differently about all of humanity. Using these insights into how vicious modernity can be and has been is at least one way to tell a different story of its successes and failures.

Therefore, some art that is forged within a sensibility and consciousness of Black diasporic suffering, resistance, and ongoing expressions of diasporic life reminds us of the unfinished business of modernity, its viciousness, and its promise. This art tends to make central to its narrative the ongoing business of liberty, freedom, citizenship, nation, and equality. In this way, many of the important ideas and desires of modernity come under scrutiny, under suspicion, and into question, particularly ideas of nationhood and citizenship. I am suggesting that it is from the place of instability that diasporic interventions, especially interventions through art, can constitute a form of universal insight. Black Canadian plays can be said generally to engage such concerns.

Since one of the central tenets of modernity is the constitution and legitimation of the nation-state and its citizen members, diasporic plays, as I am characterizing them, seem also to take as central to their articulation concerns about nation and belonging. The ongoing tensions around how Black peoples are positioned within nations, especially in regard to their citizenship, are a specific diasporic concern. Diasporic sensibilities and consciousnesses tend to make use of the ways in which Black peoples across various nations take up forms of political and cultural identification in regards to the politics of belonging. Diaspora is therefore an alternative to thinking and acting within the bounds of the defined nation.

An alternative to the metaphysics of "race," nation, and bounded culture coded into the body, diaspora is a concept that problematizes the cultural and historical mechanics of belonging. It disrupts the fundamental power of territory to determine identity by breaking the simple sequence of explanatory links between place, location, and consciousness. It destroys the naïve invocation of common memory as the basis of particularity in a similar fashion by drawing attention to the contingent political dynamics of commemoration.[6]

Many of the plays I am looking at challenge how it is that one can belong to contemporary nation-states formed from colonial and transatlantic slave histories. These plays offer an explicit engagement with belonging that opens up the aesthetic to the political and the political to the aesthetic. For example, M. NourbeSe Philip's *Coups and Calypsos* and George Seremba's *Come Good Rain* refuse the bounded culture of nation to explore a range of issues that reverberate back onto the modern nation-state and its inadequacies.

Coups and Calypsos is a play that explores the politics of race and race mixing against the backdrop of a coup. Both the political and race tensions of the play reverberate back on each other to produce various forms of instability. For if nations as imagined communities assume a particular kind of sameness, then the issues of racial, cultural, and political tensions explored by Philip expose the violence that nations must practice to produce an imagined homo-geneity. In the case of Philip's play, the historic tensions and the obvious mixing of Blacks and Indians in Trinidad and Tobago allow for an unsettling of continued assumptions that place these groups as poles apart. This destabilization of conversations does not resolve the situation but dramatically destabilizes politics, race, and culture through the race mixing and the production or evidence of the mixed-race person, in this case expressed as the dougla. Furthermore, because the main characters of the play are "of" Trinidad and Tobago but are not citizens or necessarily invested in that nation — are diasporic Caribbean of British descent — further destabilizations are evident.

George Seremba's *Come Good Rain* similarly makes use of personal memory to dramatically destabilize the inadequacies of the modern nation-state of Uganda. As Modupe Olaogun has pointed out, the play is in part based upon Seremba's escape from Uganda after his own near murder and repression in the face of what was promised to be a democratic election. For my purposes, Seremba's telling of this tale of post-colonial disappointment from outside Uganda once again points to the ways in which the ideas of modernity continue to be the basis from which a diasporic identification can be made. Exile only makes sense in the context of the production and maintenance of the modern nation-state as something that one can be estranged and removed from. The desire and failure of the post-colonial nation to produce justice for its formerly colonized citizens is a recurring diasporic desire and might constitute a diasporic aesthetic impulse. *Come Good Rain* thematizes and dramatizes the failures of the modern and post-colonial nation to live up to the promise of freedom, democracy, and liberty.

Come Good Rain is a traumatic rememory of the post-colonial nation-state's failures. In this vein it fits the diasporic paradigm that I am articulating in that its performance calls us to address the unfinished promise of modernity: the promise of liberty. The particular promise that I am referring to here is that the nation-state, especially the nation-state forged in the context of colonial struggles, was offered to Black peoples as the opportunity to participate in fashioning their own forms of liberation. Instead, *Come Good Rain* chronicles the collapse of that dream, that desire, and instead performs its falling apart. The aesthetico-political performance of *Come Good Rain* utters the diasporic desire for justice. Seremba's performance does not remain at the level of an individual narration as much as it (since it is based on his personal experience) moves beyond the individual to articulate the desires of an imagined nation and a desired justice. It therefore utters the question: what should be the ethics of a nation? The play is intended to do something. And this intention is encapsulated in Seremba's desire to have the play tour various African nations. Thus, Olaogun writes that:

> Seremba expressed his desire to tour the play in various parts of the world. He mentioned Nigeria among the places where he would like to perform.

Shortly after, Nigeria became the arena of a very repressive dictatorship under General Sani Abacha. Would a touring of *Come Good Rain* in Nigeria have made a difference? That Seremba's imaginative retelling and dramatization of his story raises a question like this one testifies to his creative and critical contributions to the important dialogues of our time.[7]

Even embedded in the critics' assessments of the play is a desire for the play to answer something about what might have happened had it toured Nigeria. One might argue that one of the central dilemmas of diasporic sensibilities and consciousness is how to articulate and perform justice and ethics. In many cases, the performance of justice and ethics is situated within a politics of what I have come to call reconnection and reparation.[8]

The Politics of Reconnection and the Instabilities of Origins

Edward Kamau Brathwaite has formulated a rather useful way of thinking about the relationship between Africa and New World Black peoples' cultural expression and performance. Brathwaite articulates what he calls "a literature of rehabilitation and reconnection."[9] Such a literature, in Brathwaite's view, is evidence of African continuities in the expressive cultures of New World Black peoples. The various expressions and performances that constitute what I reformulate as the politics of reconnection and reparation consist of: 1) Worship; 2)

Rites of passage; 3) Divination; 4) Healing; and 5) Protection. While Brathwaite is concerned with how these elements cross-reference and reinforce a continental African continuity, I am interested in how these elements appear in Black Canadian plays as the source of making reference to Africa and simultaneously finding a legitimate New World Black place in the Americas. "Reparation," in my use of the term, is concerned with making the New World a legitimate and rooted home for the expressive life of over five hundred years of Black existence in the Americas. I am suggesting that the plays under discussion here are engaged in such a project as those same plays pay homage to Africa as both an imagined and real homeland. The politics of reconnection and reparation, as I reformulate it, is an attempt to come to grips with a lost or partially remembered African past and simultaneously working through and coming to terms with the Americas as a new motherland. A number of Black Canadian plays put this actuation into performance.

Djanet Sears' *The Adventures of a Black Girl in Search of God* makes use of all five of the qualities listed above to proffer a reconnection and reparation with Canada as homeland at the same time as it references continental Africa in its various performances. First, the diasporic identification. As Leslie Sanders writes: "The theme of reclamation recurs in other ways. Throughout *Adventures*, Rainey eats dirt, a practice frequent especially among pregnant women in central Africa and the Southern United States …. The conflation of an action suggestive of pregnancy, mourning, loss, and land resonates eloquently.

At the end, her husband, Michael, too, eats the dirt from Negro Creek, signaling their rootedness and their reconciliation."[10] As Sanders so clearly points out, the play thematizes an identification with a range of Black identities as it is concerned with impacting its nationally-local — not just finding but cementing a place for blackness directly in the crevice of the nation of Canada.

Sears' use of pregnancy symbolism to claim belonging to Canada is crucially important for a number of reasons. Challenging the ongoing assumption that Black peoples are recent to Canada is the most urgent and pressing need. But additionally, as I have articulated above, the desire to reconnect and make reparation with the new homeland of the Americas as a site and home for blackness and Black peoples is a pressing and ongoing psychic concern. The ingestion of dirt not only by women in the play, but also by men, is, I would argue, one of the most central claims of making reparation. In this case, the reparation is made by claiming Canada as home with no rejection of Africa. Instead, Africa occurs in the aesthetic performances of the play. In song, dance, worship, healing, and rites of passage, Africa occurs in more abstract terms in the play's texture and gesture. *Adventures of a Black Girl in Search of God* is a play about memory, mourning, and coming to terms with loss. Consolation for the loss of Africa is negotiated through the difficult terms of claiming a new homeland, even if that homeland must be struggled over to be claimed. Sears' play offers no seductively seamless solution to the various tensions that constitute the ongoing desires of Black diasporic people in relation to the unfinished business of belonging to various homelands.

George Boyd's *Consecrated Ground* similarly fits a number of the criteria for a politics of reconnection and reparation. Centering around the destruction of Africville, Boyd's play treats the difficult belonging of Black peoples to Canada. But as a counterpoint to Sears' play, Boyd's takes up what it means to demolish the evidence of Blackness in the homeland. The trauma of Africville, as contemporary as it is, remains an open and raw wound, evidence of the violence of the modern nation-state. Africville's destruction, and Boyd's attempt through performance to place it in contemporary public memory beyond that of Black folks, is crucial to what I have been arguing. *Consecrated Ground* in its very title signals immediately the various expressive practices that constitute the politics and literature of rehabilitation, reconnection, and reparation.

To consecrate is to seek to make something sacred. In the popular imagination of nations, many sites and moments come to mark the sacred as an emblem of national cohesion and identification. Boyd's play seeks to make Africville sacred in the Canadian popular imagination, to make art do something. But such an attempt is also in keeping with the various ways in which, both at the macro and the micro level, forms of ruling and governing become central to reordering life so that other moments might become evident and have some impact on our humanity. A brief example from *Consecrated Ground* is in order:

Sarah

Gov'ment give 'em a license. The gov'ment don't put no plumbin' in here. Why the gov'ment put all the coloureds here in the first place? No jobs 'cause the gov'ment. (*beat*) Now you think Sarah Lied truss the gov'ment? You think any coloured person in he's right senses truss the gov'ment and they signs?[11]

This short discourse on the government, and Black mistrust of it, can be read in a number of ways. The actual destruction of Africville, which was the work of government, points to both the ways in which, at the micro level, governments are deeply implicated in subordinating Black people. But also, for my purposes, at the macro level it is about how practices and processes of governing or governmentality place Black peoples in a globally subaltern position. The articulation by Sarah in *Consecrated Ground* has similar or variant utterances in all of the plays that I have discussed in this essay. But importantly, such concerns, such utterances, also prove to be the point of diasporic identification for many Black peoples.

Recently, Africville has in some ways become consecrated ground. The federal government of Canada has now made the site a national treasure. Furthermore, plans to rebuild the Seaview Baptist Church on the site might signal a particular national attempt to come to terms with the trauma that the destruction of the community *is*. The rebuilding of the church should not be given short shrift, because the church not only represents a particular cultural center of the community, but more broadly it can be read as signaling yet another one of those diasporic moments of reconnection and reparation. Embedded in the practices of the Black church are many African continuities, but also embedded in the Black church are the kernels of cultural expression that can or might constitute the basis on which reparation might be made. In short, much of the expression of the "traditional" Black church continues to produce "Africa" and the New World as mutually constitutive of the kind of blackness that I am attempting to articulate.

Conclusion: The Destabilizations of the Ethical

Finally, these plays dramatically destabilize the mythical narratives of home, nation, and citizen. Because they move between nation and diaspora, homeland and imagined homeland, they productively draw on each site for advancing a politics and an aesthetics of strategic universalism. From the point of view of the dispossessed, the subaltern, these plays are intended to *do* something. I am suggesting that these plays are intended to represent the world from a vantage point from which justice and the ethical might be approached. From the ongoing and central concern for articulating practices and desires for justice and ethics emerge, the strongest elements of what I have been calling diasporic sensibilities and consciousnesses. This claim can be made about a number of different plays, but what I am claiming here is that for Black diasporic plays, even those that are not the most accomplished, justice and ethics reside inside the aesthetico-political performance of the play. Each play is intended to *do* something, and deciphering what the play intends to do is part and parcel of experiencing the play. These plays don't all announce a politics or political stance, but they perform desire, a call to justice. The plays perform an incitement to approach the ethical.

I have deliberately not given summaries of the plays being discussed. What is at stake in the argument I am making is not the total story of the plays but the ways in which the plays destabilize various assumptions. The dramatic insights of these plays put into the public sphere various questions that force us to rethink a range of concerns, issues, and conditions. And even when a play is not at its most aesthetically pleasing it can still center a series of questions which force viewers to confront the unthought of living a life; in short to confront the ethical; in short to rethink the human.

Originally published in *Canadian Theatre Review*, 118, 2004, p. 99-106.

Notes

1. Wynter, "Rethinking Aesthetics," 267
2. Ibid., 269
3. Walcott, "Riotous Black Canadians," 3-5
4. Walcott, "Post-OJ Black Men," 75-77
5. Gilroy, *Against Race*, 230
6. Ibid., 123
7. Olaogun, "The Need to Tell This Story," 334
8. Walcott, "Pedagogy and Trauma," 135-151
9. Brathwaite, "The African Presence in Caribbean Literature," 214
10. Sanders, "History at Negro Creek," 488
11. Boyd, *Consecrated Ground*, 422

References

Brathwaite, Kamau, or Edward Kamau. "The African Presence in Caribbean Literature." In *Roots*, 190-258, Ann Arbor: The University of Michigan Press, 1993

Gilroy, Paul. *Against Race: Imagining Political Culture Beyond the Color Line*. Cambridge: The Belknap Press of Harvard University Press, 2000.

Olaogun, Modupe. "The Need to Tell This Story: George Seremba's Narrative Drama *Come Good Rain*." In *Testifyin': Contemporary African Canadian Drama, Vol. 1*, edited by Djanet Sears, 331-335. Toronto: Playwrights Canada Press, 2000.

Sanders, Leslie. "History at Negro Creek; Djanet Sears' *The Adventures of a Black Girl in Search of God*." In *Testifyin': Contemporary African Canadian Drama, Vol. 2*, edited by Djanet Sears, 487-489. Toronto: Playwrights

Canada Press, 2003.

Walcott, Rinaldo. "Riotous Black Canadians." In *Testifyin': Contemporary African Canadian Drama, Vol. 1*, edited by Djanet Sears, 3-5. Toronto: Playwrights Canada Press, 2000.

———. "Pedagogy and Trauma: The Middle Passage, Slavery and the Problem of Creolization." In *Between Hope & Despair: Pedagogy and the Remembrance of Historical Trauma*, edited by R. Simon, S. Rosenberg, C. Eppert, 135-152. Lanham: Rowman & Littlefield Publishers, Inc, 2000.

———. "Post-OJ Black Men." In *Testifyin': Contemporary African Canadian Drama, Vol. 2*, edited by Djanet Sears 75-77. Toronto: Playwrights Canada Press, 2003.

Wynter, Sylvia. "Rethinking 'Aesthetics': Notes Towards a Deciphering Practice." In *Ex-Iles: Essays on Caribbean Cinema*, edited by Mbye Cham, 237-279. Trenton: Africa World Press, Inc, 1992.

Chapter 2

Multicultural and Creole Contemporaries: Post-colonial Artists and Post-colonial Cities

A city must remain open to knowing that it does not yet know what it will be.[1]

[T]he city increasingly mediates circuits of political engagement and cultural reproduction at a post-national scale of analysis. It is important politically because the city becomes the disruptive force in the reproduction of cultural and political form, the mediating field through which newness comes into the world after the cosmopolitan loses its populist gloss.[2]

Introduction

September 11, 2001; March 11, 2004; and July 7, 2005 mark significant moments for cities at the beginning of the twenty-first century. The events that made the cities of New York, Madrid, and London leak into each other in ways that would not have been evident before is buttressed by a narrative of fear and terror that has come to dominate numerous city spaces in our new colonial present.[3] More than any human geography, the city has become the dominant site in the Western imagination with its accompanying narratives of threat and fear in the Age of Global Terrorism and virus-fueled pandemics of all kinds, such as HIV/AIDS, SARS, avian flu, and Ebola. The intimacies of city life have always carried a narrative of fear and threat and thus a constant lurking danger or violence. The city also has been a place of possibility, experimentation, and the pleasure of anonymity, coupled with the promise of something "to come." The triumph of the Age of Global Terrorism and viral pandemic hysteria is that discourses of the city as a site of danger have become dominant in our times. That danger has become the prevailing metaphor and trope of the city requires that we pay careful attention to how this moment has come to be and how it organizes contemporary forms of human life since most of human life happens in cities.

We must think of the narratives of the city as central to the interventions that left or progressive scholars working in the humanities, social sciences, and spaces in between can make to what we might call (hijacking a phrase from David Scott), the new "problem-space" of the city. Scott describes the problem-space as "conceptual-ideological ensembles, discursive formations, or language games that are generative of objects, and therefore questions."[4] To think of the city as a new "problem-space" is to make sense of the city as a space and place that "must remain open to knowing that it does not yet know what it will be," as Jacques Derrida[5] puts it. I turn to Scott and

Derrida in accounting the city because I intend to suggest that the city is the site where critique as a continued strategy for living a life becomes possible.

This chapter concerns itself with thinking of the city and multiculturalism as sites for the productions of "new forms of human life."[6] or a human to come. It makes sense of the ways in which artists and theorists whom I term post-colonial have reimagined and reproduced the city as a space of desire and as "a democracy to come."[7] In this chapter, I focus on the works of Dionne Brand and Stuart Hall. In the case of Brand, I am interested in metropolitan artists in post-colonial spaces who produce art meant to do something. The perspective that art is meant to do something does not deaestheticize art; rather, it suggests that the aesthetics of art are political scripts and narratives of a kind. My attention is on moments or fragments of artistic insight that allow us to glimpse into the "to come" of the city that might act as counternarratives to the ongoing utterances of life's complex intimacies. Artists offer us evidence of the past and present with a sensibility of a future-possible — a process.

I begin the chapter with the recent traumas of Western metropolitan cityscapes because it has become difficult to think of the city without thinking about 9/11 and its after-effects. Since that moment, the city has come to be marked as a new site of a coming tragedy, a tragedy that appears to be more imaginable than at any time before. The hole left in the ground where the World Trade Center towers stood seems to stand in for the new contestations of city life and living. At this moment, reading Michel de Certeau's "Walking in the City" might give one an eerie experience and sensation. The essay's aerial view from the 110th floor of the Word Trade Center offers a vantage point from which the ruins of the Twin Towers bookmark the old and a contested coming anew of New York landmarks. de Certeau's essay seeks to map the city as a space analogous to the act of speech, and thus walking in the city comes to mark a kind of speech act. The enunciative aspects of walking in the city in our new speech moment bring fear, threat, and suspicion of other walkers. The other walkers, many of whom are migrants to metropolitan city spaces, are inscribed with the mark of threat and danger as well as hyperrealized with the mark of terrorist and/or polluted viral carrier. The poetics of an intimate and possibly political resonance of city life is characterized by the viciousness of modernity's most powerful invention: the city. As Derrida teaches us in "(No) More Rogue States":

> However much one may try to contain the effects of September 11, there are many clear indications that if there was a trauma on that day in the United States and throughout the world, it consisted not, as is too often believed of trauma in general, in an effect, in a wound produced by what had effectively already happened, what had just actually happened, and risked being repeated one more time, but in the undeniable fear or apprehension of a threat that is worse and still to come.[8]

It is the still to come that sits at the foundation of the ongoing narratives of threat and fear that continue to shape our common world. One of the central apprehensions of the worst still to come is the place of the post-colonial migrant within the metropolitan city. The fear and threat have been proclaimed as an end to multiculturalism. But I argue that the task for scholars is that we need to struggle with the idea of multiculturalism, for Stuart Hall tells us "we have no better terms to think the situation with."[9] I also suggest that we need to up the ante in the struggles around the idea of multiculturalism and offer something more, something that is simultaneously empirical, imaginary, and to come. The something I offer is creole-ness.

Cities and the End of Multiculturalism

In an episode of the television show *Will & Grace*, Grace hires an identifiable (or at least we are to believe so from the name and look of the person and other references) Middle Eastern woman to work in her design firm. Grace hires her not because she is the most qualified but because Grace wants to right a wrong.[10] The character of the Middle Eastern woman is played over-the-top so that her Middle Eastern name is extremely long, there is an assumption of gender victimization, and a dislocated sense of place and racial discrimination are offered as central markers of the woman's experience. These assumptions produce the desire in Grace to right a wrong through the act of hiring her. The woman turns out to be a horrible employee, even worse than Karen (which those familiar with the show will know to be quite significant). But Grace's intent to right a wrong does not allow her to fire the new employee. After losing her best client because of the employee's incompetence and finding out that the woman is Jewish, Grace finally acts. Grace proclaims to the woman how pleased she is to learn that she is Jewish because Grace is Jewish, too. After the two women bond very briefly, Grace fires her, stating that she cannot discriminate against her own and that she will see her now former employee at prayers. Such is the resolution to Grace's dilemma of hiring the wrong person and regaining her client. I found the episode a curious statement on contemporary fears and threats as well as the proclaimed demise of multiculturalism.[11]

Grace's desire to right a wrong by making an offer of employment is understood by her as an act that her Western metropolitan privilege can make available. Western liberalism as the savior of victimized others, especially by their own kind, becomes the underlying theme. However, her claim that she cannot discriminate against her own makes use of a shared but differentiated Jewish-ness to undermine the altruism of her act. The act is ultimately embedded in a multiculturalism that makes us all the same. Such enactment of the politics of difference is not the kind of ethnopolitics that I am hinting at. The comedic moves in *Will & Grace* function to undo the political impact of identifying a wrong that can be righted but is obscured by our commonalities. This should not be surprising since the show's entire run has been about a sexless gay man who becomes so normalized on heterosexual terms that we can tolerate him since he is just like one of "us" only with a few gay quirks.[12] An assumed uncomplicatedness of belonging, identity, and even nation becomes the grounds of regulation, containment, and refusal. But when one sits outside of these grounds, there can be no doubt that identity comes to the fore again.

There is much more that can be said about the *Will & Grace* episode, but I am more interested in how we got there in the first place, and how the demise of multiculturalism can make any kind of sense in this historical moment. I am interested in the heuristic claim of demise because it is a claim that, if made unintelligible, might allow for a moving away from the narratives of threat, fear, and danger that have become dominant in our post-colonial times. The numerous discourses of multiculturalism might be understood as an inadequate but necessary compromise of post-colonial and post–civil-rights eruptions and their moderate success in providing new forms of human life in the West. In the historical present, or our new colonial present, those who have historically been colonized experience both hyperimperialism and the older, vulgar colonial practices that target largely but not exclusively those whom the threat, fear, and danger narratives are meant to confine, control, and contain.

In this regard, the cities of the metropolitan West are not just multicultural, that is cities constituted of racial, ethnic, and cultural differences, but are also post-colonial in the sense that they are a break with the regime of earlier moments of colonial arrangements in condition and in figuration. Both former colonizer and colonized now occupy the same geopolitical space. The multicultural, for me, is one index of the post-colonial condition of anticolonial and neo-colonial utterances and desires, of a global post-colonial to come. It is only, in fact, through the arrivals and departures of the colonial venture, both old and new, that a global post-colonial to come is possible. Thus, the assault on the nascent appearance of a post-colonial to come as encapsulated in the claim of a demise of multiculturalism in the post-9/11 world is much more in line with older versions of colonial and imperialist orders than with the newer versions of the global financiering of the world, a neo-colonial condition called the New World Order, the Age of Global Terrorism, or globalization. Such names obscure the ongoing workings of colonial practices in which we conceptually apprehend overlapping colonial conditions of old and new.

As Stuart Hall points out concerning the forced migrations caused by various upheavals:

> Migration is the joker in the globalization pack …. In the new globalization everything moves with a new fluidity: capital, investment, goods, messages, images …. Only labor — people — are supposed to stay still …. Nevertheless, against the grain of the system, the second half of the 20th century and the first years of the 21st have seen an un-precedented explosion of the largely unplanned movement of peoples.[13]

The unplanned movements of people have arrived by and large in metropolitan places and reconfigured those spaces as something other than their conventional history suggests when new arrivals bring with them and make immediately present other histories that had been subjugated and/or discredited. Multiculturalism is, then, both the containment of such histories and their excess. It is not too much to claim that the desire to see a disappearance of multiculturalism as a desire for a post-colonial to come is shrouded in a need to reaffirm and replicate older and newer forms of colonial and imperialist mechanisms of authority and military biopower. Much of the new colonial and imperialist authority and energy are expended on limiting migration and its impacts. To engage Hall's assessments again:

Migration constitutes a disruptive cultural force within globalization. Unlike earlier phases, where the problems of religious, social, and cultural difference were held at a safe distance from the metropolitan homelands, contemporary migration intrudes directly into, disturbs, challenges, and subverts, metropolitan cultural space. It projects the vexed issue of pluralism and difference into the settled monocultural spaces of the Western metropolis. It has produced an epistemic rupture, generating the thematics of a new problematic — that of the post-colonial moment.[14]

One of the central emergent narratives of the new marking of the city is the proclamation of the death of multiculturalism. But a truism is in order: cities are by their very nature multicultural. So what kind of multiculturalism is over or being referred to (or "referenced") in claims of its death? The kind that is being named as dead, and rightly so, is state multiculturalism. What I am suggesting is that it is our responsibility to keep alive and relevant the idea of multiculturalism. The idea of multiculturalism is central to how we might live the intimacies of post-colonial cities and their migratory conditions and politics. The idea of multiculturalism helps us to make sense of how post-colonial cities come to be and how the state has responded to the historical positioning of the phenomena of living colonial, post-colonial, and metropolitan crimes or crimes of the ongoing colonial order simultaneously. The idea of multiculturalism is one that both conceptually and pragmatically grapples with the fact that culture, ethnicity, and race are meaningful categories to many people and have become the basis upon which they organize themselves into voluntary and forced collectivities. The idea of multiculturalism acknowledges the fluid and in flux nature of claims based on racial, ethnic, cultural, and other differences as never static but always in a process of unfolding tensions and possibilities.

Since the end of the Second World War, metropolitan places in the West have been pedagogically preparing for the threat and fear that have come to characterize our present. The riots of Notting Hill and Nottingham in the 1950s; the civil rights movement; the women's movement;

the antiwar and antinuclear movements; the post–civil-rights fires of the Black cities of the United States and thus the production of the burnt-out ghetto inner city; the gay and lesbian movement; the race riots of the 1970s and 1980s in Britain; the Reagan/Bush years of heightened security characterized by racialized helicopter surveillance of Black and Latino communities; heightened immigration border controls; and the production of the fear of refugees have been contained by the discomforting politics of state multiculturalism that sought to curb struggles for a democracy to come. Out of these movements and politics has come the political context from which the multicultural idea, and thus the state multicultural compromise, sprang. The state multicultural compromise might be characterized by the state's attempts to fix identity markers as the basis of its multicultural policies. Such fixing could not allow for fluidity and the constant changes that occur in a multiculture; thus, in moments of crisis the multicultural compromise fails to hold as a pack that is capable of resolving difficult questions and concerns. The compromise has been called into question by many as identity politics, and has produced a scholarly impasse of essentialism and antiessentialism that jettisons the ethico-political and the ethnopolitical in favor of unmasking shoddy political claims based upon struggles over state power. Now is the time to think of state power again and to think of it in the context of the ethico-political and ethnopolitical, both ethics and ethnicity/identity. We need to be vigilant not only about how state power positions us in political terms but also about how new paradigms of ethnicity are being positioned within and across states. The machinery of citizenship, ethnicity, and nation has resurfaced (if it ever did go away) in ways that we must urgently re-engage.

The most recent manifestations of the overlapping history are the murder of Theo van Gogh in Amsterdam; the bombings in London, England; the riots in France's *banlieues*; and the continued intra-Black and other forms of minoritized violence in North American cities. The tremors of the continuing post-colonial and post–civil-rights crises tell much about the unfolding of overlapping colonialisms ushered in by the neoliberal global reordering within the terms of mobility of finance capital and a de-centered global production line. The above outbreaks, to use language from the viral pandemic, are only symptoms of a much larger malaise. Let me take as an example the claims being made concerning the bombings in London.

The shock, or the worse to come, to return to Derrida, of the London bombings centers on the identification of the bombers as British Muslims. The assumption is that they should have been counted on to be loyal to the nation. The shock is that they were not loyal to the state, that they had reoriented themselves to what has been termed a fundamentalist perspective of the world, and that their "new" homeland (for it is always new for such bodies) was at odds with "their" ways of knowing and being. The condition of being at odds, which, if we follow Fanon[15], is the condition of the colonized, was meant to be apprehended by various incarnations of state and corporate multiculturalism, a multiculturalism meant to salve the wound of colonial and post-colonial displacement and dislocation and persistent racisms in the West. Bringing some identifiable members of marked racial and ethnic groups into the field of consumption and/or as representable models of capitalist success was and is meant to demonstrate that entering the circles of the elite nation always remains possible. The youth, both symbolically and literally, are supposed to demonstrate that one does not have to leave anything of their "cultural selves" behind to enter the realm of the elites. The shock is that state multiculturalism was supposed to produce forms of being that made use of anthropologized and objectified culture and cultural practice as the basis upon which second- and third-generation youth born of British colonial adventures would come to be contained in Britain. That the anthropologized cultural objectification of the other's culture failed to contain, but might have succeeded in other ways, in this case to produce a radical, if perverted, sense of resistance, is the moment of crisis in the announcement of the failure of multiculturalism. In that sense, state multiculturalism has failed and so it should. But the idea of multiculturalism is one that we must nonetheless continue to work with.[16]

The failure is in the state's inability to quell the conditions of diasporicity, migrant subjectivities, and racisms of all kinds. The migrant subjectivities that continue to be the form and condition through which second and third generations of post-colonial subjects live their lives in the metropolitan space are of crucial necessity for us to consider. If the allegations of the London bombings are correct, what we are faced with is the stunning defeat of state multiculturalism as we witness it being unmasked within the conditions of our new colonial present. The colonial present is coterminous with a new imperialism that seeks to control the movement of peoples and to reconstitute identity, nation, and ethnicity as conditions for a politics of suppression of the creole conditions of metropolitan human life. The actual story in the much-vaunted announcements of the demise of multicultural-ism across Europe and North America is grounded nei-ther in empirical evidence nor in the imagination. The attack is really launched at the idea of multiculturalism and the creole present it can bequeath us. Thus, we might think of the bombing of London as one of the difficult moments of creolization since we can never just think of creolization as a happy story, even though it is also a story of possibility.

The claim of the demise of multiculturalism, then, only functions in regard to state multiculturalism and the policies that flow from such regulation. There are many kinds of multiculturalism, but the evidence of a lived and everyday multiculture does not disappear in the face of metropolitan elites decrying and claiming the demise of state multicultural polices. Instead, the everyday and banal multiculturalism that we live in intimate urban spaces functions as the backdrop for a move toward a more creole experience.

Creole Cities: A Post-colonial to Come

The last scenes of Isaac Julien's 1991 film *Young Soul*

Rebels offer a glimpse of a community to come as the white, the Black, the male, the female, the gay, and the heterosexual come together dancing to African-American music, having formed a new and more hopeful affiliation within the context of racism and nationalism of the 1970s. The moment of affiliation in the film comes from a recognition of differences and a political solidarity based on a poetics of relation within and across national and psychic boundaries. Julien captures the changing relations of race, nation, gender, and sexuality as the substance of what Hall[17] terms as "new ethnicities." The moment of new ethnicities that Julien cinematically represents is what I call everyday or popular multiculturalism. It is a multiculturalism that occurs from below, driven by the intimacies of urban life. It is also a multiculturalism on its way to creolization. Creolization is the result of multiple differences and their intimate encounters producing "mutual mutations"[18] as the point toward further and more opacity in terms of cultural formations, expressions, and articulations. It is only possible in a multiculture. The film utters the imagined and material context of multicultural London at that time. The images of a differently racialized and ethnicized London in the post–July 7, 2005 moment utter yet another one. They are the creole children of the racism and nationalism that Julien's film calls into question. They are the creoles of London, now misrecognized as fundamentalists of all sorts.

The development of creole society, as Kamau Brathwaite calls it, results in a society "caught up in some kind of colonial arrangement with a metropolitan European power."[19] Brathwaite writes about the Anglo-Caribbean and in particular Jamaica when he offers that definition. He suggests that creole society is a complex situation where external metropolitan forces pressure the colonial polity to make constant internal adjustments between master and slave, elite and laborer, and so on "in a culturally heterogeneous relationship."[20] I contend that many of Brathwaite's terms for the conditions of creole society also manifest themselves in the metropolitan space, especially in conditions concerning cohabitation and uneven acts of power. Thus, Brathwaite's definition requires a bit of fine-tuning when relocated elsewhere. Before I offer that fine-tuning, let me be clear that creolization takes place in the context of unequal and brutal power arrangements alongside forms of severe cultural dominance. As Hall points out, creolization could not take place without extensive transculturation. It arises out of the brutal context and unequal power relations through which differing cultures come into contact and engagement with each other. In the period of transatlantic slavery and its aftermath, the early state of the plantation society and the state of our times have been the arbiter of uneven power and its brutalizing qualities. The importance of creolization as a term to think with is its location between brutality and something different, something more possible, if I can use such a phrase, the fusing and mixing of cultures forced to cohabit together that renders something else possible.[21] Humanists and social scientists must think of new possibilities and enter empirical and imaginary evidences into the public sphere and the public debate of our new realities.

The *longue durée* of multicultural metropolitan spaces has been in the midst of a creole process for some time now. Most city spaces are creole places even if we don't think of them in those terms. In *Times Square Red, Times Square Blue*, Samuel Delany plots one moment of creole sensibility in New York City prior to its Disneyfication. He articulates a sexual community whose existence is both marginalized and demolished by the remaking of Times Square as a middle-class playground. What is powerful about his observations and analyses is that he understands what is missing: the comingling of people across race, class, and culture through sexual desire and practice. In one of Delany's central claims about the city, he writes:

> I propose that in a democratic city it is imperative that we speak to strangers, live next to them, and learn how to relate to them on many levels, including the sexual. City venues must be designed to allow these multiple interactions to occur easily, with a minimum of danger, comfortably, and conveniently. This is what politics — the way of living in the polis, the city — is about.[22]

The politics of city living has been chronicled by a significant number of artists from the former colonies and of the disposssessed in the West and by their descendents. I am interested in artists who have constituted a migratory subjectivity in relationship to transatlantic slavery and colonial history because I believe that such artists bring a unique position to articulating the city. In the Canadian context, no contemporary artist has consistently grappled with the city and its multivalent contours like the poet, novelist, and essayist Dionne Brand.

Brand has been writing about the city as a material and imagined place since 1983 with her *Winter Epigrams and Epigrams to Ernesto Cardenal in Defence of Claudia*. Over that time, the city has changed and evolved from a cold and frigid place to one in which alienation, celebration, pain, shame, and pleasure live up close to each other. Brand's poetry, fiction, and essays chronicle a history of the evolving cityscape of Toronto since the 1970s. For instance, a relatively recent essay in *Brick* magazine reflects on the joys and pleasures of women's boxing at a local Toronto gym where she attended to witness a friend's debut in the sport, a sport that has become a lesbian underground practice in many major cities.[23] She chronicles the economies of city living with a language evocative of the tight spaces we negotiate. Her conception of the city is different from where I began with *Will & Grace* in that Brand's city is not one where elites right wrongs but rather where the ingredients of creole-ness are realized in what Glissant[24] terms as the "unimaginable turbulence of relation." The multiculturalism of Brand's city embeds the violent intimacies of everyday life, state practices, and the hopefulness of living together in moments of mutual recognition that are the signs that provide movements and thus possibility for something else to come into being. In "Thirsty," Brand[25] writes:

> History doesn't enter here, life, if you call it that
> on this small street is inconsequential,
> Julia, worked at testing cultures and the stingy
> task, in every way irredeemable, of saving money
>
> Then Allan came, his mother, left, came ill
> squeezing a sewing machine into a hallway
> and then the baby. Already you can see how
> joylessness took a hold pretending to be joy

The poem "Thirsty" comes out of the tragedy of a police shooting a black man in the early 1980s. Brand does not vindicate; she offers a reading of the city in which entanglements of pain and beauty might signal one response to the traumas of the place. She writes of Toronto as a "city that had never happened before." But if we bring Brand's uttering into conversation with Derrida, we have generations of cities since all cities suffer the condition of having not happened before. "Thirsty" is a poem very local in its articulations, a kind of eulogy to Toronto, but much wider in its impact and call to an ethics of living together in a community of which we might demand an ethico-political in accord with a Derridean hospitality to the stranger.

In "Land to Light On," Brand is more pensive about the city. The poem might be read at first as a disappointment in and refusal of the nation-state as a place of ethical belonging. She gives up on land to light on, declaring, "I don't want no fucking country, here, there or all the way back." She moves to the hyperimmigrant local of Toronto to call nation and world into question and to demand an ethical accounting of the pain of movement. Thus, "Land to Light On" is dedicated to making sense of how movement facilitates a particular kind of politics.

In Brand's essays and short stories, the same kind of attention is paid to the city as the locus from which to view and engage a larger politics concerned with the international ethico-political and ethnopolitical. Anyone familiar with Toronto as a space and place would not be surprised why one of Canada's best living poets would find such inspiration in Toronto. In *What We All Long For*, Brand writes Toronto like it has never been written before, and maps places, spaces, and people like a cartographer's poetics denuded of its science. The novel monumentalizes Toronto through the ordinary and the everyday. Brand works with a notion that the city has never happened before, and thus, her narration is in keeping with the "to come" aspect that I have been delineating. Her novel is in fact a counterpoint to the neoconservative desire to have multiculturalism disappear as though these conditions are only possible in state announcements and legislation. In fact, *What We All Long For* ushers in the creole city.

The characters in the novel are a group of twentysomething young people of color who resemble the kinds of folks accused in the London bombings. They either have migrated to the city at a very young age or were born of first-generation migrant parents for whom their children's cultural difference is both shared and confusing. But this is not a novel about generational conflict. It is about migrant subjectivity even when there is no place to return as is the case for the second generation and after. It is a novel about how cultural difference is lived as a moment, as something else to come. Brand neither celebrates nor denounces multiculturalism; she writes its possibilities and outcomes. One of its outcomes is a creole sensibility or condition with the vicious pleasures that such entails.

Let me focus on one strand of the novel. The novel concerns itself with various reasons why migration happens. It also allows me to advance the idea of how violence is a central aspect of seriously accounting for our multicultural present and its process toward a creoleness to come. A central strand of the novel concerns the character Quy, who is the brother of Tuyen, a young aspiring artist. Quy is lost by his family when they flee Vietnam in the 1970s. Quy does not hold onto his mother's hand strongly enough, and she loses him as the refugees run to the boats. Quy makes his way to Thailand, where he becomes part of the underworld and eventually makes his way to Toronto. Quy's mother is inconsolable about her loss, and his sister Tuyen wishes for Quy's return so that she might be given the space for self-expression in a family with strict demands for the youngest girl child. Tuyen is neither Vietnamese nor Canadian; she is her very local self, more captured by the poetics of the urban than by any national geography or imaginary.

For much of Quy's life, he is stateless, calling to mind certain aspects of Agamben's insights on the place of law and no law.[26] Quy is the kind of refugee who sits in a wasteland contained by law but in which no law can speak on his behalf. The place of law without law has recently been hyperactuated in legislative bodies like the US Homeland Security department and the security certificate program in Canada, but refugee claimants find themselves at such junctures more so now. Quy's fate from the tragic evening in Vietnam has been to exist below the radar of state-organized human life.

Through a series of events, Tuyen discovers Quy's existence in the city. She approaches him and arranges for him to meet the family. While waiting outside the family home, Quy is apparently murdered for his car.[27] Quy's death at the hands of a stranger, but one familiar to his sister, is a moment in the novel where the politics of a creole to come announces its most brutal aspects. In the novel, Brand is not romantic about the city; she writes its violence and joys, its pain and laughter, its sorrow and fruit. The city is not a locus of resolution; it functions as the place where resolution might be possible. The intimacy of living close and living together can act as the conduit to a different kind of conversation. I suggest that our task as scholars is to make that conversation happen better than it has been happening.

The tragic circumstances of Quy's apparent death act as one of the conditions through which the multicultural space and place of Toronto is not romanticized. The textures of Brand's narration of Toronto's cityscape recoil with his death, and simultaneously propel the cityscape forward as new knowledge, new ways of being, and new relations are found in the aftermath. There is no single aspect of Brand's novel that makes it utter the deep textures of Toronto's creole sensibility and form. Its textures, both thick and thin, pervade the work and, in its most hopeful ethnographic sense, give the reader a sense of what pervades the landscape and the possibilities to come. In this sense, creolization is a process toward what Sylvia Wynter[28] calls "new forms of human life." How might scholars think of these new forms of life to come? The elements of the novel that move us toward the tragedy of the violence that Quy encounters allow us to apprehend how those who know each other in the aftermath will be forced to plot new ways of being in the world they intimately inhabit — a move toward a creole reality. The new modes of being can only be but accessed as new modes of human life in the aftermath of the violent reconfiguration of knowing and living a life together.

Conclusion: New Forms of Human Life

The urgencies of our new colonial moment have found scholars searching for rehabilitating and resuscitating concepts of all kinds to think of these new conditions. No other concept has made a firmer return than cosmopolitanism.[29] Let us take Kwame Anthony Appiah as our example. In *Cosmopolitanism: Ethics in a World of Strangers*, Appiah asks under what rubric to proceed in this moment. He answers: "not globalization" and "not multiculturalism." In my view, Appiah creates a false separation between multiculturalism and cosmopolitanism. Each idea inflects the other, and thus, it is not possible to have one without the other. What Appiah fails to do, but which he does better in *The Ethics of Identity* although he does not go far enough, is to think about the state. The idea of multiculturalism, as it has been entangled in state and corporate discourses, pollutes it no more than cosmopolitanism's colonial history. So why not multiculturalism? I think it is the overall frame that Appiah's uses, one that produces an inability for him to challenge state power explicitly and one that he precedes from that reduces the idea of multiculturalism down to only state and corporate multiculturalism. He finds in the history of cosmopolitanism more to work with but does not recognize the state and corporatist reduction of the latter to the language of global citizen. What is significant, for me, about Appiah's arguments in *Cosmopolitanism* is that his examples approach what I have been calling creolization. However, his fear of ethnicity does not allow him to go there. By his fear of ethnicity, I mean that, in every instance in Appiah's text where ethnicity rears its head as a meaningful attachment, his practice is to argue that it is a faulty idea. I argue, however, that the move is not to undermine such passionate attachments but rather to point out how the attachments are in a long process of movement and possibility elsewhere. To approach the situation from the place I am suggesting, one cannot fear ethnicity as a problem, but one must embrace it as a meaningful and yet not fully possible marker of self and collectivity.

When we think of these ideas in the context of the city, we recognize what Michael Keith points out: "the city increasingly mediates circuits of political engagement and cultural reproduction at a post-national scale of analysis. It is important politically because the city becomes the disruptive force in the reproduction of cultural and political form, the mediating field through which newness comes into the world after the cosmopolitan loses its populist gloss."[30] Thus in cities (and elsewhere), ethnicity and its claims are both a crutch and a lever toward something other and something more in conscious and not-so-conscious ways.

The ethnopolitical is important because we must confront the ways in which the new colonialism and imperialism continue to make identity a locus of control, containment, and regulation. The recent pass of a knee-jerk identity politics critique has now reached its conclusion, meaning that we can no longer make the claim that identity does not matter and that it is far more the problem than the resolution of problems. Previous critiques of identity politics too easily dismiss appeals to identity in an effort to mobilize a politics that might move beyond self-recognition into one that might activate a practice of care for those with whom we did not share anything in common. The critiques of identity politics that many of us quickly fell victim to shifted the politics of the dispossessed. But in the post-9/11 world, identity has re-emerged as a function of the state to mark, contain, surveil, and incarcerate in a fashion that requires a serious re-engagement with identity claims.

In the post-identity politics moment, the only stable category that those of us on the left had was class. It was a curious moment, for clearly we did not do the work to make the interventionist politics of various identity groups garner real traction. Such is particularly evident when class, which is heavily racialized in the spaces I have been discussing, is reproduced in our studies as a kind of empty category in which the "real problem" of identity, race, is not essential to understanding it. In much of left humanities and social sciences, class has become a signifier of a transcendent identity category: it is an identity without an identity, and race and culture only enter to sully it. The ethnopolitical is not an appeal to essentialize identity, but rather to highlight the ways in which identity especially ethnicity, matters in our colonial present. As Diana Fuss stated back in the heady days of the essentialist/constructionist argument, "To insist that essentialism is always and everywhere reactionary is, for the constructionists, to buy into essentialism in the very act of making the charge; it is to act as if essentialism has an essence."[31] I am not making a case for ethnopoliticality as the only ground of a renewed collective politics, but I am arguing for the language of ethnicity as a central element for how we approach a collective politics of the possible and thus a post-colonial to come, out of our present multicultural and submerged creole present.

Finally, it will have been noticed that much of the conceptual scaffolding of my argument has been built through artists and intellectuals who have a relation of some sort to a region we call the Caribbean. I would not want such attention to be interpreted as chauvinism, but I do want to place on the conceptual agenda a piece of potentially difficult knowledge. The archipelago of poverty, as Wynter calls it, is a place that has produced an interesting and arresting relation to modernity, both within and against it. Most Caribbean people are people who must make themselves native to a place they are not from. Caribbean people also occupy a place that drove the engines of the modern industrial world, and play a significant role in migratory practices to the former and now new again colonial powers. The unique place of the Caribbean as extension of Europe, Africa, and Asia; as amputation and extension; as overseas department; as import and export; as slave, free, indentured, and in-between; as backyard of the United States makes it a place where the cosmopolitical takes root in all the messiness that ethnicity brings with it. I suggest that it is the utter uniqueness of the place and the ways in which it struggles to live both the ongoing moments of creolization and a democracy to come in the backyard of new empire and our new colonial present that has much to offer us as the people of that place continue to "quarrel with history."[32]

Originally published in "Multicultural and Creole Contemporaries: Post-colonial Artists and Post-colonial Cities" in R. Sintos- Coloma (Ed.) 161-177, *Post-colonial Challenges in Education.* Peter Lang, 2009.

Notes

1. Derrida, "Generations of a City," 17
2. Keith, *After the Cosmopolitan*, 188
3. Gregory, *The Colonial Present*
4. Scott, *Refashioning Futures*, 8
5. Derrida, "Generations of a City," 12-27
6. Wynter, "1492: A New World View," 13
7. Derrida, *Rogues: Two Essays on Reason*, 86
8. Derrida, "(No) More Rogue States," 104
9. Hall, "Conclusion: The Muticultural Question," 209
10. See Spivak (2004, 2005) for a discussion on human rights and metropolitan understandings of how they might participate in the righting of wrongs
11. For those interested in what Will and Jack were doing in this particular episode, they were having a *Brokeback Mountain* moment at a gay cowboy bar in the city
12. While the chapter makes reference to a number of queer artists and queer texts, it is not interested in queerness as a privileged identity. In fact, it argues that queer identity claims are only one among others in the present multicultural arrangements of human life. What is often important about queerness when it is asserted is that it operates at a number of in-between and bridging positions that work to make more visible the limits of other identity claims
13. Hall, "Creolization, diaspora, and hybridity in the context of globalization," 195
14. Ibid., 196
15. Fanon, *Black Skin White Masks*
16. Hall, "Conclusion: The Multicultural Question," 209-

241

17. Hall, "New ethnicities," 441-449
18. Glissant, *Poetics of Relation*
19. Brathwaite, *The Development of Creole Society in Jamaica*, xv
20. Ibid., xvi
21. Hall, "Creolization, diaspora, and hybridity in the context of globalization," 193
22. Delany, *Times Square*, 193
23. Brand, "Manos de piedras"
24. Glissant, *Poetics of Relation*, 138
25. Brand, *Thirsty*, 7
26. I draw on Agamben to point to how "states of exception" position people in precarious relation to the state. In his rendering of how the law works in such situation, the law is simultaneously upheld and under erasure. Such a position produces a kind of "no man's land" or sets up those caught in the gaps of law with no recourse to law
27. It is not entirely clear that Quy dies; what is clear is that great violence has occurred. Violence is a constitutive element of the process of creolization, which must be dealt with if creole-ness is to be acknowledged as constitutive of a difference process after the encounter
28. Wynter, "1492: A New World View," 13
29. Paul Gilroy in *Post-colonial Melancholia* favours the term "conviviality" rather than "cosmopolitanism." Gilroy's term is important in part because it recognizes the element of living together. Nonetheless, it is faulty

because it does not allow for thinking of new modes of being in the context of living together as an emergent site of new possibilities

30. Keith, *After the Cosmopolitan?* 188
31. Fuss, *Essentially Speaking,* 21
32. Glissant, *Poetics of Relation,* 61-97

References

Agamben, Giorgio. *State of Exception,* translated by Kevin Attell. Chicago: University of Chicago Press, 2005.

Appiah, Kwame Anthony. *The Ethics of Identity.* Princeton: Princeton University Press, 2005.

———. *Cosmopolitanism: Ethics in a world of strangers.* New York: W. W. Norton, 2006.

Brand, Dionne. *Land to Light On.* Toronto: McClelland and Stewart, 1997.

———.*Thirsty.* Toronto: McClelland and Stewart, 2002.

———. "Manos de piedras." *Brick Magazine 76* (winter), 2005.

———. *What We All Long For.* Toronto: Vintage Canada, 2005.

Brathwaite, Kamau. *The Development of Creole Society in Jamaica, 1770-1820.* Oxford: Clarendon, 1971.

de Certeau, Michel. *The Practice of Everyday Life.* Berkeley: University of California Press, 1984.

Delany, Samuel Ray. *Times Square Red, Times Square Blue.* New York: New York University Press, 2001.

Derrida, Jacques. "Generations of a City: Memory, prophecy, responsibilities," translated by R. Comay. In *Open city: Alphabet city no. 6,* edited by John Knechtel, 12-27. Concord: House of Anansi Press, 1998.

Derrida, J. *Rogues: Two essays on reason.* Stanford: Stanford University Press, 2005.

Fanon, Frantz. *Black Skin, White Masks.* New York: Grove, 1967.

Fuss, Diana. *Essentially Speaking: Feminism, nature and difference.* New York: Routledge, 1989.

Gilroy, Paul. *Post-colonial Melancholia.* New York: Columbia University Press, 2005.

Glissant, Édouard. "History, histories, and stories." In *Caribbean Discourse: Selected essays,* translated by J. M. Dash, 61-97, Charlottesville: University of Virginia Press, 1989.

Glissant, Édouard. *Poetics of Relation.* Translated by Betsy Wing. Ann Arbor: University of Michigan Press, 1997.

Gregory, Derek. *The Colonial Present.* Oxford: Blackwell, 2004.

Hall, Stuart. "New ethnicities." In *Stuart Hall: Critical dialogues in cultural studies*, edited by David Morley and Kuan-Hsing Chen, 441-449. London: Routledge, 1996.

——. "Conclusion: The multicultural question." In *Un/settled multiculturalisms: Diasporas, entanglements, transruptions,* edited by Barnor Hesse, 209-241. London: Zed, 2000.

——. "Creolization, diaspora, and hybridity in the context of globalization." In *Créolité and creolization: Documenta 11 platform 3*, edited by O. Enwezor, C. Basualdo, U. M. Bauer, S. Ghez, S. Maharaj, M. Nash, and O. Zaya. Ostfildern, Germany: Hatje Cantz, 2003.

Keith, Michael. *After the Cosmopolitan?: Multicultural cities and the future of racism.* London: Routledge, 2005.

Scott, David. *Refashioning Futures: Criticism after post-coloniality.* Princeton: Princeton University Press, 1999.

Spivak, G. 2004. "Righting wrongs." *South Atlantic Quarterly 103*(2/3) (2005) 523-581.

———. "Use and abuse of human rights." *boundary 2, 32*(1), 131-189.

Wynter, Sylvia. "Rethinking 'aesthetics': Notes towards a deciphering practice." In, *Ex-Iles: Essays on Caribbean cinema*, edited by Mbye Cham. Trenton: Africa World, 1992.

———. "1492: A new world view." In *Race, discourse, and the origin of the Americas: A new world view*, edited by Vera Lawrence Hyatt and Rex Nettleford. Washington: Smithsonian Institution Press, 1995.

Chapter 3

Into the Ranks of Man: Vicious Modernism and the Politics of Reconciliation

As it became both popular and influential, the political idea of human rights acquired a particular historical trajectory. However, the official genealogy it has been given is extremely narrow. The story of its development is often told ritualistically as a kind of ethno-history. It forms part of a larger account: the story of the moral and legal ascent of Europe and its civilizational offshoots. Blood-saturated histories of colonization and conquest are rarely allowed to disrupt that triumphalist tale.

Redress, from this position, becomes a public responsibility that looks forward to a healing of the democratic system — and, by implication, of the nation. By situating violated "citizens" inside the nation, the brief portrayed Japanese Canadians not as "victims" but, more significantly, as agents of change.[2]

The politics of identity in the 1970s brought

an unprecedented paradox into their lives …
From being social pariahs of the 1940s, "Japanese
Canadians" were now reborn as model "citizens,"
whose rapid upward mobility in the aftermath
of the mass uprooting demonstrated their loyalty
to the nation.[2]

What does a critical post-colonial commentary on human
rights look like? What does such a commentary in the
colonial settler nation-state of Canada look like? And
indeed, what kind or kinds of humans are at its center?
This essay proposes that the dominant mode for thinking
about human rights as a significant feature of
contemporary life has now been popularly and even
intellectually reproduced primarily as a consequence of
the Second World War. Thus, the 1945 Universal
Declaration of Human Rights is widely understood to
follow in the wake of the tragedies of war and ethnic
cleansing in mid-twentieth century Europe. However, I
want to propose that the context of nation-state
apologies to the indigenous peoples of Turtle Island
(hereafter Canada) and the desire for reconciliation
reference a much longer history of struggles for human
rights that are simultaneously the foundation of the 1945
Universal Declaration and the evidence of a vicious
modernity that cemented the European conception of
Man as if it was indeed the only way to conceive of being
human in the world. The impetus of my argument is to
point to the ambiguity of the practice of apologies and
its resultant politics of reconciliation. My claim is that

reconciliation requires a wholesale rethinking of the contemporary stakes of human life for the last 400-plus years.

Susan Buck-Morss has written that the understanding of Western modernity is always problematically formulated if questions of transatlantic slavery are excluded from it.[3] One might amend her insights to add indigenous colonization, attempted genocide, and in some cases genocide. Drawing on the case of Haiti, Buck-Morss demonstrates and argues that Western political philosophy failed to implicate slave labor in the colonies and indigenous colonization at the exact same time as the Enlightenment discourse of freedom as "the highest and universal political value" was being produced by Enlightenment thinkers. She asked how such a blind spot was possible. And further still, how is it that such a blind spot continues to be perpetuated today? What Buck-Morss' questions reveal is that the afterlife of European colonization has as it backbone or foundation the colonization of the Americas, with its near genocide and genocide and its enslavement of Africans as both its material and intellectual inheritance. Buck-Morss' claims pose a significant problem for how the politics of reconciliation is understood and practiced in late modern Canada, which must be understood in light of its embedded history in the colonization of the Americas, European global expansion, and the ways in which the ideas of coloniality continue to shape its governing and ordering of geo-political space, people, and institutions.

To fully appreciate the problematics of Buck-Morss' insights, I turn to the Caribbean philosopher, or rather philosopher of the Americas, Sylvia Wynter to delineate the ways in which European inventions of Man ordered the world and set up the terms of being human for which nation-state apologies are a tactical acknowledgement of having done wrong and at the same time are premised upon the perpetuation of "European genres of the human," invented in their attempt to rule the globe from a perspective that is entirely within their conception of what the globe and being human means.[4] Wynter has consistently attempted to make sense of the invention of the Americas or the New World as a problematic of our contemporary global humanity.

In an intellectual project that seeks to make sense of how a post-Columbus globe is reshaped on the terms of shifting European consciousness, Wynter details a *religio-secular-politico-cultural* complex, crossing a range of intellectual fields, which articulates how the White, the Red and the Black, as types or genres come to be. These genres of Man's human others — in this case the Red, and the Black are the infra-humans, that is not yet human, or only partially human, of which contemporary apologies are meant to signal their pathway into the ranks of Man. Wynter argues that these categories or types of man were invented in the moment of a hybrid European colonial domination that produced "the Indio/Negro complex," which was later transformed in a *degodded* Europe to "the nigger/native complex."[5] Wynter suggests that such designations point to how Europe's conception of Man, which "overrepresents itself as if it were man itself"[6] is one of the most difficult material and conceptual political, cultural, and philosophical issues facing us today. The end of formal colonialism does not produce any relief from European dominance of what being human might mean and be. Wynter tests her claims in the region of the Caribbean, which has also been the site of Europe's laboratory for its encounters with its invented genres of Man's human others, and in particular its encounters with the question of freedom and unfreedom as Buck-Morss so skillfully points out concerning Hegel and Haiti, the former having theorized his master/slave dialectic at exactly the same time that the Haitian revolution was headline news in Europe's papers and cafes.

If we take Wynter and Buck-Morss seriously, then the question of what constitutes European modernity is a complicated story of genocide, slavery, ecocide, and most strikingly, the production of a new world, not just for those colonized and enslaved but for those engaged in the project of expansion as well. The New World moniker is thus not a sentimental or history-denying term but references the brutal realities of life in the Americas as the bedrock of European modernity and its satellite campuses like Canada. The Enlightenment's naming and ordering of peoples, places, and things has bequeathed to us those namings and orders as the very terms through which it might be challenged. The Haiti revolution of 1791-1804 took up liberty as its central rallying cry from the same French Revolution that sought to crush it. In our time we have become Black and Aboriginal, among other names we have been forced to take on and internalize out of the very cartographies of Europe's global expansion since the fifteenth century. It is appeals to these genres of European Man that apologies are meant to assuage. The question we are often faced with is how to make other conceptions of being human and of traversing the globe appear. What intellectual, political, and cultural — not to mention economic — space do different conceptions of human life have to offer our present globalized, networked humanity? In my view, the politics of reconciliation throws these questions up without offering answers. One is thus left asking what is being reconciled, with whom, and to what?

Reconciliation suggests a past action. It suggests that some wrong has been done for which the possibility of forgiveness is an act of coming together again. Reconciliation suggests a significant rupture of some kind has occurred. Above, I have suggested that European colonial expansion from the fifteenth century onward produced a rupture in the Americas, which in part produced the settler colonial nation-state of Canada, which also produced new states of/for being indigenous peoples and belatedly African peoples. Those kinds of collective namings — indigenous, African, Indian, Asian, even European — are the cataloguing evidence of the historical rupture for which European Man comes to overrepresent itself as if it was indeed Man. As Paul Gilroy suggests, the "[b]lood-saturated histories of colonisation and conquest are rarely allowed to disrupt that triumphalist tale,"[7] one that apologies and the politics of reconciliation attempt to make invisible in the contemporary moment. Thus reconciliation also suggests a certain kind of suturing is possible in the aftermath of the brutalities that makes it a necessary response in the first place. But what reconciliation does not appear to do is to dismantle the institutional basis of the present arrangements of human life. Reconciliation does not ask us to rethink where we are at. It asks us to accept the present as an accumulation of injuries for which apologies must suffice as the entry into the flawed ecocidal, genocidal, anti-human, late modern world still premised on Europe's partial conception of the human as the only option for being human in world. Does reconciliation provide us a view towards a new or more hopeful humanism?

For the immigrant population coming out of the Caribbean who, under the rules of European modernity, had to make themselves "native to a place they were not from,"[8] and whose histories of enslavement and colonization entangle in complexly creative and maddening ways with indigenous cultures of the Americas, the nation-state of Canada, and Europe's imperial powers — past and present — apologies and reconciliation marks the perversity and viciousness of modernity and its incomplete promise of human liberation. For the former slave, indentured laborer, and the hybrids of all sorts in the "archipelagoes of poverty"[9] the struggle to be human is one conditioned by the terms upon which European discourses could both be internalized and turned upside down to produce them as subjects worthy of being considered Man, if only tangentially so. The struggle against Atlantic slavery, especially in imperial Britain, is now understood as the first actual global human rights struggle. The brutalities of African slavery and indigenous resistance to life-altering colonial expansion are indeed the bedrock of what is now a neutered human rights discourse emptied out of ideas which sought to fundamentally and radically rethink what human life might mean.

It is my contention, then, that the politics of reconciliation only matter to the extent that such practices tell the alternate and much more disturbing story of global capitalism's apparent triumph and concurrently of the attempts to resist it and undo its impacts in the past, present, and future. What is at stake is an exercise, which tells the tale of the cost of European expansion as one which is bigger and more brutal than the myth of Europe's conception of the world being the only valid idea of human life and a myth that must continually repress ideas of living differently in many pre-contact cultures that remain with us still.

I have written elsewhere that Black/African diaspora discourses, or the stories of those not fully human in Europe's terms, matter because such discourses are the B-side to the celebratory narratives of globalization (especially in the academy) now offered as the triumph of Europe's vision of a global humanity.[10] In this view, the brutality of diaspora narratives temper and offer other indices of globalization's history and its impact, as well as its present, so that modernity's vicious charms may be unmasked and its consequences laid bare. Black/African diaspora narratives, then, are about the historical unfolding of Europe's run at global domination, but they are also about the continuous refusal of that domination by various global forces since its inception. Significantly, Black/African diaspora narratives are also about the making of meaningful lives within the context of Euro-Western Enlightenment and modernity — both as products of it and crucially as resignifiers, inventors, and originators of what can only be described as discrepant modernities for those who have borne the brunt of Europe's expansionist practices.[11] In essence, it might be argued that those produced in the crucible of the New World are truly *the* modern people. What I am trying to stress is that the Atlantic region, with its history of territorial theft, transatlantic slavery, and genocide, is the *incubator* of a set of conditions which we have inherited as a global situation organized on the basis of Euro-Western traditions of thought and the human, and from which we must figure out how to extricate ourselves. A sober conversation about what that extrication means will account for political economy, cultural borrowing, sharing, mixing, and its outcomes and impacts — contradictory and otherwise — and our entangled histories of power, knowledge, and land. I am not sure that apologies and the language of reconciliation take us there, but as a Western and modern subject, I am also not prepared to throw it away just yet either. This is the ambivalence that I signaled above.

One of the central claims of European Enlightenment and modernity was to make a better human, but such desires were premised on making some not-human and then only admitting them into humanity, sometimes partially so, based solely on models from Europe's perspectives. Grappling with such a history would prove useful and powerful as a central aspect of the politics of reconciliation because it is in fact the various ways in which deployments of Western conceptions of the human function that continue to be the basis from which desires for reconciliation are meant to rescue us collectively. In the case of "new world" for Indigenous and Blacks specifically, reconciliation can only be but a beginning towards a much more profound and challenging discussion and institutionality of what it means to be human that rests upon the multiple perspectives of human-ness in which European concepts are but one among many. Reconciliation is a beginning; unimagined transformation is the desired outcome.

Originally published in *Cultivating Canada: Reconciliation through the Lens of Cultural Diversity*. Mathur, A., Dewar, J. and DeGagne, M. (ed.). Aboriginal Healing Foundation: Ottawa, 2011, 341-350

Notes:

1. Gilroy, *Darker Than Blue*, 234
2. Roy, *Redress*, 310
3. Buck-Morss, "Haiti and Hegel."
4. Wynter, "Unsettling the Coloniality of Being/ Power/Truth/Freedom: Towards the Human, after Man, Its Overrepresentation—An Argument." CR: *The Centennial Review*
5. Wynter, "The Pope must have been drunk, the King of Castile a madman: Culture as Actuality, and the Caribbean Rethinking Modernity," 27
6. Wynter, "Unsettling the Coloniality of Being/ Power/truth/Freedom: Towards the Human, after Man, its Overrepresentation—An Argument"
7. Gilroy, 55
8. Kincaid, "Flowers of Empire"
9. Wynter, "Rethinking Aesthetics: Notes Towards a Deciphering Practice"
10. Walcott, "Salted Cod ...: Black Canada and Diaspora Sensibilities."
11. I am using the term "Euro-Western" to signal the ethno-centered organization of what we have come to call the West. It is a term meant not only to signal Europe but also those satellite settler colonies like the USA, Canada, Australia, and New Zealand who understand themselves to be Euro-Western in founding and organization. However, as much of my argument suggest or implies, the West itself is now so complicated that it would be a conceptual problem to take "new world" Black people out of it. Thus, "Euro-

Western" works to anchor the particular discourses that I am addressing here to a Europe that, at a certain historical moment, understood itself as mono-ethnic insofar as its expansionist project was concerned

References

Buck-Morss, Susan. "Haiti and Hegel". *Critical Inquiry*, 26, no. 4 (2000): 5.

Gilroy, Paul. *Darker than Blue: On the Moral Economies of Black Atlantic Culture*. Cambridge, MA: Harvard University Press, 2010.

Kincaid, Jamaica, "Flowers of Empire". *Harpers Magazine*, April 1996.

Miki, Roy. *Redress: Inside The Japanese Canadian Call for Justice*. Vancouver: Raincoast Books, 2004.

Walcott, Rinaldo. "Salted Cod...: Black Canada and Diaspora Sensibilities". Thames Art Gallery, 2006.

Wynter, Sylvia. "The Pope must have been drunk, the King of Castile a madman: Culture as Actuality, and the Caribbean Rethinking Modernity". *The Reordering of Culture: Latin America, The Caribbean and Canada, In the Hood*. Ottawa: Carleton University Press, 1995.

Wynter, Sylvia. "Unsettling the Coloniality of Being/Power/truth/Freedom: Towards the Human, after Man, its Overrepresentation—An Argument". CR: *The Centennial Review* (3.3), (2003): 257-337.

———. "Rethinking Aesthetics: Notes Towards a Deciphering Practice". *Ex-Iles: Essays on Caribbean Cinema*, edited by Mbye Cham, Trenton, New Jersey: Africa World Press, 1992.

Chapter 4

Disgraceful: Intellectual Dishonesty, White Anxieties, and Multicultural Critique Thirty Years Later

Introduction: The Legacy of Europe's Global Reign

The events of September 11, 2001 appeared to have solidified a consensus on multiculturalism: until that moment, multiculturalism in its state form had been settled policy. In this essay, I argue that such claims are patently false and are more indicative of white anxieties post-9/11 than of any previous multicultural consensus. Not only has state multiculturalism always been a contested policy but also the very idea of multiculturalism itself has always been and will continue to be a contested idea. Western liberal democracies like Canada adopted various forms of state multiculturalism to manage and neutralize post–World War II struggles for social and economic justice by racial and cultural minorities, and to constrain the movement of mainly non-white migrants into national spaces, which had formerly imagined, represented, and performed themselves as entirely white. State multiculturalism sought to contain such "uprisings" through policies centered on identity and culture while maintaining and retaining the power to authorize and legitimize the late-capitalist material relations of the nation-state. However, continual upheavals in state multicultural rhetoric have meant that even the state has often revised its idea of multiculturalism, and thus its policy, in response to competing ideas about what multiculturalism is and what it should do.

I am therefore suggesting that one cannot fully make sense of post-9/11 multiculturalism debates without taking into account the context of Western global expansion over the last five hundred years — a period in which Europe reordered the globe under its own terms or ways of knowing as the only legitimate way of being. More specifically, the making of the Americas, especially settler colonies like Canada, and the invention of the modern nation-state in its current liberal democratic form, are all clearly implicated in the conversation. The implication comes through the discourse and language of freedom, which has been the basis of contestation for the last five hundred years for a range of different groups and or peoples since it was not freedom as understood in its context for all. The post-9/11 claim that multiculturalism is over represents a kind of intellectual dishonesty that refuses to take seriously both state reforms and compromises in the context of peoples' resistances to being managed — it is indeed an ahistorical claim.

In this post-9/11 world, pundits have attempted to enshrine liberal democracy as the only system that guarantees human freedom and emancipation.[1] Such a willfully impartial rewriting of liberal democratic ideals is interesting since to do so, one must conceal the brutal forces of unfreedom, which made freedom an ideal for others in the first instance. The pundits have thus refused to engage the history of human dreadfulness upon which liberal democracies of the West have been founded — all of them instituted through enormous acts of violence. As Toni Morrison reminds us in *Playing in the Dark*, "the slave population, it could be and was assumed, offered itself up as surrogate selves for meditation on problems of human freedom, its lure and its elusiveness."[2] She also adds, "we should not be surprised that the Enlightenment could accommodate slavery; we should be surprised if it had not. The concept of freedom did not emerge in a vacuum. Nothing highlighted freedom — if it did not in fact create it — like slavery."[3] With New World slavery and Aboriginal colonialism, which constitute the foundations of the Americas as we presently live them, as evidence, Morrison's comments bring home the point that while five hundred years of European global hegemony has cemented one version of what freedom is, other ideas of freedom still remain among us.

In her discussion of Hegel and Haiti in the pages of *Critical Inquiry*, Susan Buck-Morss attempts to reanimate the debate concerning modernity and its discourse of freedom. She argues that Western political philosophy has failed to grapple with the implications of slave labor's spread in the colonies at the exact time that the Enlightenment discourse of freedom as "the highest and universal political value" was being produced by

Enlightenment thinkers.[4] She further asks how we can, in our times, produce this same blind spot, if it is indeed a blind spot and not an intentional act in our scholarship. And, she cautions us not to place the counterevidence of what Paul Gilroy once brilliantly called "the counter-cultures of modernity" as simply belonging to someone else's story, that is the story of non-white peoples only.[5] Buck-Morss wants us to mix it up, so to speak.[6] What she documents and demonstrates is the centrality of unfreedom to Europe's now–realized global ambitions and aspirations, especially in Euro-American terms, as those terms moved from Europe as a declining colonizer to the USA as a new imperial power. Her challenge is to forms of intellectual dishonesty, as I call them, by some Western academics and pundits who refuse to acknowledge the troubled origins of European ideas of freedom, nation, and democracy.

The impact of Buck-Morss' argument is to make clear that the afterlife of European colonization of the Americas has silenced the evidence that Indian genocide and near–genocide, as well as African enslavement, form the backbone of European modernity — both materially and intellectually. Both Sibylle Fischer and Michel-Rolph Trouillot have built on Buck-Morss' position in their reading of Haiti's 1791-1804 revolution (or more accu-rately its culmination) as central to the emergence of the central tenets of European political philosophy and liberal democratic states.[7] European philosophy had to ignore, write against, and collude with practices of unfreedom, which lay at the source of its very making. Thus, the epistemological violence inherent in European political philosophy is not new but rather takes its imprimatur from a history of intellectual practice that has always looked the other way, as Buck-Morss excellently points out. This is especially so in the present moment when scholars in the social sciences and humanities are struggling to think through the current global situation. In this instance, the idea of multiculturalism has been negatively racialized and bears the brunt of liberal philosophy's disdain.

I suggest that in a post-9/11 world, a re-engagement with European modernity's genres of the human is required. This re-engagement must negotiate a number of overlapping and contradictory flows and contexts, and must simultaneously recognize that there are no guarantees, and that for politics to happen, there must be a "symbolic drawing of the boundary; there has to be some symbolic divide," as Stuart Hall puts it.[8] In the "eventful moment" of 9/11, then, Bush was right about one thing: the "us against them." The "with us or against us" of his rhetoric produced the necessary and important arbitrary closure to proceed to war and to further harden global capital in its neoliberal guise with the aim of re-ordering the world. While Bush's early comments produced this arbitrary closure for certain conditions of neoliberal ideologies to unfold globally in relation to a civilizational divide, the rhetoric found its legitimacy in public intellectual debates, popular culture, policy debates, and a range of other contexts under which post-Columbus European expansion ordered life globally and could thus proceed as if it were natural, normal, and the law. But such hegemony has always been challenged. The post–World War II uprisings by racial minorities in the West and by colonized peoples stand as examples of how states could be remade and even produced in the aftermath of those contests.

The Idea of Multiculturalism and State Multiculturalism

Multiculturalism as an idea is a central element of the new, post-civil-rights social movements, the post-colonial "racial contract," as Mills terms it, of the second half of the twentieth century and the beginning of the twenty-first.[9] In this instance, it is a racial contract premised on European modernity's categorizations of people who have, over time, come to genuinely take those categories as both serious and meaningful to their lives. The multicultures of Europe's imaginary now play a role in defining and redefining what culture might mean; thus, the idea of multiple cultures coexisting is now a fixture of our times. This role also has to be understood in light of the massive movements of peoples across geopolitical spaces, constituting new modes of living and new forms of social life. In some abstract ways, these new modes of human life and sociality might also be conceived of as multiculturalism.

One of my central claims in this chapter is that state multiculturalism borrows from the idea of multiculturalism and redirects it as a tool of the state. State multiculturalism is invested with the power to manage a range of differences that might potentially prove troubling in a hegemonic state's bid to retain its exclusive authorizing powers. The idea of multiculturalism provides avenues for living with difference that do not always have to obey coercive state power. Thus, the idea of multiculturalism allows for forms of social relations that take difference as central to human existence, not as a problem but as a set of creative and non-coercive ways to approach living life to its fullest potential. Indeed, the idea of multiculturalism shares with liberal democracy the ideal that human beings can reach beyond themselves to fashion a world of social good valuable to all. Yet post-9/11, the negative side of multiculturalism has been accentuated.

These days, everyone has something to say about the failures of multiculturalism as both an idea and as policy. We can find these comments in the unlikeliest of places. David Cronenberg, discussing *Eastern Promises,* his film about the Russian mafia and the smuggling of young Eastern European girls as sex slaves, is quoted in *The New York Times,* stating:

> When you have a culture that's embedded in another, there's a constant tension between the two … In the US the melting pot was supposed to mean you come and you absorb American values. But in Canada and England the idea of multiculturalism was something else. At its worst it's you come and you live there, but you live in a little ghetto of your own culture that you brought with you. I supposed

that's happening in the States with the Spanish language. Can multiculturalism really work? I don't know, but it's an interesting study.[10]

The article proceeds to tell us that Cronenberg recalls growing up in a mainly Jewish Toronto area which was repopulated by Italians as the Jews moved north. He recalls hearing Dean Martin through walls "and learning about Fellini from an Italian-Canadian boy. 'That's the good part of multiculturalism,' he said. 'That's the dream of it. The bad parts are the animosities brought from other countries.'"[11] Cronenberg's comments on multiculturalism are interesting, not the least for the ways in which they demonstrate that the popular intellectual debate concerning multiculturalism has penetrated all kinds of realms.

While *Eastern Promises* dramatizes the trafficking of women across various borders, it is in no way about traveling/migrating antagonisms from Russia to England; rather, the antagonisms are internal to the migrants (and perhaps even generations of migrants). Cronenberg's reference to the ethnic, cultural, and/or linguistic ghettoization of the Spanish language in the US is equally interesting since he was speaking as a Canadian who is presumably familiar with Canada's two official languages. What, then, was he trying to say? In talk like Cronenberg's, a certain kind of symptom — the symptom of the racialized other — becomes more easily visible. This specter of the racialized other, invented in the moment of European expansion and solidified in its modernity, with its systemic categorizing of people, places, and things, continues to structure our contemporary world. Indeed, it is this categorization that drives state multiculturalism along with its management and containment strategies.

Thus, in 1971, when Pierre Elliott Trudeau introduced Canada's multiculturalism policy, the opposition leader, Robert Stanfield, rose in the House to emphasize that the policy in no way changed the character of the Canadian nation as constituted by two founding peoples. This understanding of Canadian nationhood has been reified in a range of state practices such as the bilingual nature of the nation and even in some measures of citizenship and access such as the Queen of the United Kingdom's continuing position as the nation's head of state. Similarly, in the 1980s, when the Mulroney government — implicated in the unfolding of neoliberal arrangements, such as beginning the dismantling of the welfare state in Canada — shifted multiculturalism from a policy to the Constitution Act, it was attempting to maintain state arrangements while benefiting from the new and ongoing migrations that are so central to Canada's capitalist economic health (I mean migrations both planned as in immigration and unplanned). What is important to recognize in both the announcement of the policy and the further creation of the Act is that the idea of multiculturalism remained contested even among Canada's elites. Since 1971, multiculturalism as policy and practice in Canada has been contentious from a range of political ideologies and positions. Any suggestion otherwise is an ahistorical suggestion that is, quite frankly, disgraceful and intellectually dishonest.

And yet, in the last few years, the Canadian public has been engaged in a debate concerning multiculturalism, citizenship, war, and terrorism, which fails to engage the history of either the policy or the idea of multiculturalism. Articles in the popular media by Allan Gregg (pollster), Michael Bliss (historian), Janice Gross Stein (political scientist), and Cecil Foster (sociologist) have all contributed to this debate in significant ways.[12] Importantly, Stein's essay "Living Better Multiculturally" sparked both kudos and criticism in *The Globe and Mail* and the *Toronto Star*. *Globe and Mail* columnist John Ibbitson praised the essay, while *Toronto Star* columnist Haroon Siddiqui quarreled with it.[13] Stein's essay suggests that multiculturalism, and cultural rights by extension, runs counter to the best practices of liberal democracies. But she goes further to suggest that multicultural policies might in fact harm liberal democracies and render them relative states. It was the responses to Stein's article — laudatory and critical — that pointed out to me the need to engage more actively with both the interpretation of Canadian multicultural policy and the larger question of the idea of multiculturalism in a post-colonial world.

Gregg, Bliss, Stein, and Foster all assume that the idea of multiculturalism has been settled in Canada, yet all but Foster believe that the nation's comfort with multiculturalism requires reassessment and/or renewed endorsement. Certainly, the substantive changes we have witnessed globally require a renewed discussion of multicultural policies. However, I would argue that Canadian multiculturalism as policy, practice, and even as an idea has never been settled. Further still, I believe that Canadian multiculturalism has been a useful instrument in the unfolding of neoliberalism insofar as it has prompted various ethnic communities to support political parties that appeal to their ethnic interests, for example. And yet, at the same time, the circulation of the idea of multiculturalism in the Canadian public sphere offers the possibility of other logics to emerge.

So, for example, Cecil Foster praises Canada for its multicultural accomplishments with tongue in cheek, suggesting that the queen of Canada is now Black since Nova Scotia's Lieutenant-Governor Mayann Francis and the Governor General Michaëlle Jean are both black women. However, many anti-racist scholars and pundits on the political left would argue that such appointments demonstrate a toothless practice of multiculturalism that does not adequately support the transfer of power to racialized Canadians; this is one of the earliest anti-racist critiques of state multiculturalism. And yet, in another article, Foster argued that in Canada, multiculturalism has made race irrelevant and thus any discussion of Toronto Muslims plotting acts of terror ought not to be cast in terms of a critique of multiculturalism but rather in terms of whether Canada desires to make race an essential element of its citizenship again.[14] What is interesting about Foster's claim is that many others — yes, anti-racist scholars and activists but left critics too — would argue that race always remains a salient element of Canadian citizenship.

In a different vein, Michael Bliss, Janice Stein, and Allan Gregg all argue quite earnestly that multiculturalism is at odds with Canadian social values since its hijacking by various religious and cultural fundamentalists. In their view, most of these fundamentalists are a multicultural array of non-white Canadians. For Bliss, Stein, and Gregg, Canada is undermined as a nation by its unwavering support for the idea of multiculturalism and our collective faith in the policy and the Constitution Act to produce a common basis for the practice of citizenship. How might we make sense of these different positions held by these public intellectuals? Is Foster correct that race no longer matters? Or are Bliss, Stein, and Gregg right in claiming that disunity and uneasy partnership characterize the polity? Can partnership be assumed from our present social relations? And for whom are all those folks writing?

In fact, Foster's rather rhetorical and romantic claims can be traced to bureaucratic interpretations of the policy and the Constitution Act. The Department of Canadian Heritage, where the multiculturalism program is located, historicizes multiculturalism as having evolved over at least three different phases: cultural preservation and celebration (the Trudeau period); inclusion and anti-racism (the Mulroney period); and social cohesion (pre-9/11 period). Thus, even at the level of governance, understandings of the policy and the idea are not settled. From this perspective, engaging with the policy and the idea of multiculturalism carries new and important political imperatives, since a new multicultural logic is always possible. I am not of the school of thought that multiculturalism is an entirely useless idea; rather, I am conscious of it as producing what David Scott terms "a problem-space" from which new kinds of questions must emerge so that different kinds of answers and, more importantly, different kinds of desires might surface.[15]

In this regard, *Uneasy Partners: Multiculturalism and Rights in Canada*, a collection of essays by a group of elite public intellectuals claims to offer new questions about the multiculturalism debate.[17] What this collection of essays actually does is pursue old arguments that have been well worked over by scholars and intellectuals, many of whom I engage with below. What is particularly interesting, however, is that none of the numerous scholars who have spent significant time engaging with these issues are cited or discussed in the book. Such patent intellectual dishonesty is, in my view, part of the reason why the debate on multiculturalism in this country is one that has posed no new questions for the idea of multiculturalism. While at least three of the contributors to the collection count Canadian multiculturalism as a success, even those essayists fail to question the racial contract of which state multiculturalism is such a fundamental element.

The essays gathered in *Uneasy Partners* speak into an assumed void, which does not and has never existed. As I have pointed out, there exist now more than thirty years of scholarship and debate concerning Canadian multiculturalism. What *Uneasy Partners* actually does is to establish who the legitimate spokespeople on the question of the future of Canadian multiculturalism might be. With its requisite contrarian (Haroon Siddiqui) and its cheerleader (John Meisel), the book is mainly concerned with propping up the idea that multiculturalism in Canada runs counter to liberal democratic rights and that it implies the provision of those rights. Well, some of these folks believe that multicuturalism policy is a good example of liberal democratic rights and others believe it messes with those rights. I have argued elsewhere that this is hardly the case and that the idea of multiculturalism must be thought of as a part of rights discourses and in fact, even further as collective rights discourses, pushing the boundaries of what we think liberal democratic states and their citizens can be accountable and responsible for. *Uneasy Partners* is fundamentally concerned with a reassertion of white hegemonic pronouncements on the continuing and future status quo of the Euro-American "right" to determine the future of the state and thus of human life. To do so, it must both ignore more rigorous scholarship and invent itself *tout court*. It must also simultaneously co-opt what appears to be opposition to its claims by including the evidence of dissenters. In short, this book is an example of the racial contract par excellence.

Most recently, Cecil Foster has written two books on multiculturalism: *Where Race Does Not Matter* and *Blackness and Modernity*. While I have fundamental conceptual differences with many of Foster's claims, it is curious that he has not garnered more attention in the debate. As faulty as Foster's claims might be, and I think they are, he argues against a tribal view that would guarantee white and some racialized elites the intellectual and political apparatus to manage the nation-state. He recognizes them as a tribe when they would rather be unmarked as such and mark others instead. Foster writes,

> The last laugh of the jester would be heard in the 1960s, when Canadians decided that their country would be officially raceless. When they decided to make theirs the world's first officially multicultural country, Canadians were tapping into a view that had always been part of the Canadian body politic; they were harking back to the universalism and humanity that Lord Simcoe had epitomized.[18]

Foster then offers a further explanation in which Lord Simcoe's opposition to slavery is understood as recognition that "Canada was not exclusively European."[19] Further still, he claims that the evidence of this lies in the gift of Caribana to the Canadian nation-state, a celebration which falls on Simcoe Day, which is also Emancipation Day in the Anglo-Caribbean. The main problem with Foster's claims is that he very clearly overreaches. Simcoe's opposition to slavery was progressive for its time, but it by no means signaled Canada as a non-white colonial nation-space. In fact, emigrationism was an important part of his anti-slavery stance. Similarly, contemporary multicultural policy, as I have stated above, is in no way a challenge to the national myth of Canada as a white nation-space or a raceless state. In fact, multicultural policy is arguably an acknowledgement of the racial state and is in essence a racial contact that binds the arrangement. My point here, however, is not to prove Foster incorrect, but to point to his interpretation of multicultural policy as one that must be ignored, lest it pose too many questions for Stein et al, who are hell-bent on whipping up hysterics about the multicultural threat. It does not take many difficult hermeneutic maneuvers to detect that race-talk is the foundation of their multiculturalism threat.

Significantly, in the last thirty years or so Peter Li, B. Singh Bolaria, Enid Lee, Barbara Thomas, Roxana Ng, Augie Fleras, Himani Bannerji, Richard Day, Eva Mackey, Sherene Razack, and a range of other scholars, activists, and public intellectuals like NourbeSe Philip, Dionne Brand, and Neil Bissoondath, have offered a range of political perspectives and positions on multiculturalism. It would be entirely impossible to sythesize these authors' various and divergent positions. This is, in part, the point I am making. None of these people have been engaged in the most recent debates (even though Penguin Canada rushed Bissoondath's book back into print). Nonetheless, these perspectives have played a central role in how Canadian multiculturalism is understood in diverse circles. Thus, it might be argued that the only consensus on Canadian multiculturalism in the last thirty-plus years is that it has become a fundamental Canadian entity, but a consensus on what it means and how it should work continues to elude us. Ideas and practices of multiculturalism remain contested sites and so they should be. If multiculturalism is at all an element of what might constitute new forms of social cohesion in an era that appears to be, at least rhetorically, balkanized, then thinking and struggling over what it might and could mean is a useful and productive endeavor. Stuart Hall's claim that migration is the question of the twenty-first century is crucial to this conversation. In my view, , migration cannot be thought outside of the idea of multiculturalism and multicultures simultaneously. Hall cautions that we must struggle over the conceptual and discursive meanings of multiculturalism — a challenge for those who would throw away or abandon the concept to corporate forces and/or the political right — to come up with a better term with which to think through these conditions.

Stein et al.'s *Uneasy Partners* is framed through the language of rights, especially with regard to the state's management of its citizens. In Canada, that management takes place through the Charter of Rights and Freedoms. Interestingly, Foster's discussion of rights takes a turn toward the question of freedom.[19] Discourses of freedom are in fact a significant question for liberal democracy. Foster himself tries to address this fact but is so committed to his particular kind of liberalism that he never poses the question of unfreedom in the context of liberal democracy. It is my argument, in part, that rights, as organized by and governed through the state, might be said to actually abort a more pure freedom.

The new questions confronting both the idea and the policy of multiculturalism are centered on notions of freedom and unfreedom. We need to better understand the nature of our contemporary unfreedoms. I assert this perspective in the context of the overwhelming managerialisms of neoliberalism in various institutions and within global corporate capitalism. Neoliberalism in its many and varied incarnations is a very specific assault on freedom; or, put differently, it manages our unfreedoms through what many have come to identify as an audit and surveillance culture. Contemporary debates about multiculturalism collude with these modes of unfreedom, as well as with attempts to manage both the planned and unplanned migrations of the twenty-first century. In the context of multicultural encounters, the language, discourse, and practices of surveillance and security now occupy a crucial place in managing the movement of people around the globe.

If we take Janice Stein's "Living Better Multiculturally" as a question, what kinds of answers or new questions might we provide? Is there a place for the question of unfreedom? And if migration is now a *de rigueur* fact of human life, what would it mean to conceptualize multiculturalism as outside a narrative of arrival or, more broadly, of progress? What would it mean to instead begin to think of encounters with cultural difference as inevitable and therefore always the place from which human engagement, and thus negotiation, proceeds? It seems to me that these sorts of questions pose different concerns for the ways in which theorists are attempting to think about intensified cultural difference and movement. If we take seriously the importance of understanding that liberal democracy is founded on unfreedoms and not freedoms, as the intellectuals committed to the partial insights of European modernity and its philosophy like to proclaim, then the problem-space of multiculturalism as an idea begins to reveal itself. The revelations take us down the road of having to consider how white anxieties are framing this moment and its debates.

Disgraceful Claims and White Anxieties Post-9/11

By "white anxieties" I mean to signal a state of aggression by Euro-American intellectuals, policy analysts, and others who must now confront their ever decreasing power to have their partial view of the world appear as the only legitimate view of the world. In this new context, a kind of white anxiety has come into being, in which previous compromises are being rethought so as to preserve what can only crudely be called white power. White anxieties, in this case, are dressed up in terms of debates on rights discourses, the future of the liberal democratic state, tensions between the secular state and religion, and so on. In each case, white anxieties betray themselves in their bearers' assumption of the role of steward of the conversation, dialogue, and debate, thus positioning themselves as the protectors of the continually unfolding "freedoms" of secular liberal democratic societies. Consequently, all others, usually racialized others, become the barbarians screaming at the doors. The racial contract manages those screamers for better or worse.

Multiculturalism is both an outcome of European modernity, and its initial moving of people around the globe in ways that disrupted previous settlements of those peoples, and a political compromise of the post-World War II anti-colonial and civil rights resistances of racialized, feminized, and sexualized subjects. It is also a managerial tool used by the state against those who resist state-imposed, policy-driven differences. Migration, then, is a crucial element of modernity and not an outcome of it. At the same time, the idea of multiculturalism is attractive for the political possibilities it offers for dealing with what have now become very meaningful and real cultural differences for many. In this sense, multiculturalism, as a condition of contemporary human life, is not easily or readily overcome. Thus, Hall argues that we must use multiculturalism under what he calls "erasure," while we struggle over its meaning to arrive at a new political logic that might better address our contemporary human condition.[20]

Any new multicultural political logic must recognize the importance of hope sustaining itself in a world that seems devoid of it. But even more important than hope might be the politics of new and different utopian futures that move beyond both the failed experiments of the left and what appears to be the unstoppable machine of capitalism. The second half of the twentieth century has seen a waning of utopian futures in public discourse. Indeed, one of the triumphs of neoliberal ideology has been its very effective management of the imagination, alongside the management of the economy, institutions, populations, and so on. I want to suggest that in this era of fundamentalisms of all kinds, our inability to engage critically with new imaginative worlds, to think critically and imaginatively about liberal democracies, and/or to imagine worlds other than those we have experienced is one of the central questions that intellectuals and activists engaging with the idea of multiculturalism must pursue. That ideas about multiculturalism were so quickly marked as contentious in a post-9/11 world suggests that a certain cultural order of modernity was profoundly disrupted by the events of that day. To paraphrase Sylvia Wynter, the rupture that 9/11 marks is one which points to the ideology that the partial perspective of European modernity can be the universally valid perspective.[21] It is this that I believe has pushed the charge against multiculturalism since one of the possibilities of a hopeful multicultural logic is the unleashing of various and competing conceptions of people, places, and things. In other words, there have always been different conceptions of the human and the world; multiculturalism could subversively recognize as much. Such recognition, decidedly different from Charles Taylor's use of the term, would require different human arrangements across space and time around the globe — what he calls "recognition," which is a liberal philosophical move, echoes Buck-Morss' critique of the discipline of philosophy I began with.[22]

What one might argue is the conclusive and substantive difference between the post- and pre-9/11 world is that the struggle over the how and what of European modernity has never been so clear. Drawing on Scott's conception of the problem-space, one could suggest that much anti-colonial struggle was premised on the flexibility of the terms of modernity to absorb all kinds of difference under its terrain of freedom and equality as ever-expanding qualities enabled by admitting some who were previously left out. Their expansion seemed to be halted in the unfolding of the neoliberal global assault.

In my view, the rolling back of rights and freedoms reaches it apogee in a post-1960s world with the election of Margaret Thatcher in Britain in 1979, Ronald Reagan in the US in 1980, and similar-minded chancellors in Germany and presidents in Japan where the unfolding of very specific economic international policies alongside domestic policies produced a narrative of demonization and practices of managerialism that still occupy a central place in neoliberal practices today. Thatcher's Britain demonized Black youth, helping to produce a crisis of mugging, which continues to frame Black youth experiences in that country even now. Reagan's double term built the framework for attacks on African-American and Latino/a working classes and their communities. Through rewriting a series of laws, so-called gang violence was targeted in US urban centers, producing and reconfiguring what many scholars and activists have come to call the new slave system of the US and/or the prison industrial complex.[23] Most significant, however, are the forms of demonization, surveillance, and practices of otherization which accompanied this putatively non-economic side of the neoliberal triumph. Attacks on multiculturalism as an idea took root in public discourse and consciousness during this period.

What I am trying to get at here is that in various

geopolitical spaces the formations that now seem to be boiling over into a robust conversation about multiculturalism were well underway prior to 9/11. However, it would be a mistake to look for a sure pattern across these different spaces. The Canadian context differs from Britain's and the USA's, since both the 1970s and 1980s saw the further entrenchment of multiculturalism as Canadian national policy. During this time, in Britain, Thatcher was dismantling the very interesting experiment of the Greater London Council. Such differences reveal the contradictions of neoliberalism as a policy that should work similarly everywhere, yet does not; there is no global unanimity.

If we think of liberal democracy as a system of rules that confer various advantages upon those for whom the rules constitute a substantive portion of their cosmology, then liberal democracy becomes a system that neither produces nor provides a level playing field, as many of its intellectual defenders would have us believe. Those intellectuals would have us believe that liberal democracies are fundamentally consumed with the question of liberty and equality, or freedom. However, if one begins to place the development of liberal democracy within the context of other modes of knowing, one is forced to confront the unfreedom upon which liberal democracy's freedoms are articulated and canonized as normal. Once unfreedom is understood as an intimate and intricate element of liberal democracy, a different set of questions emerges for some of the contemporary debates we have encountered recently.

Debates such as the Danish cartoon controversy, the murder of Theo van Gogh, and the wearing of the veil and other religious insignia in public places all point to the unfreedom that frames and underpins liberal democracies; these debates are not actual aberrations from it. Liberal democracies are as much about structuring state-sanctioned unfreedoms as they are about providing reforms in relation to the constant evolution of the market and the population. Similarly, the controversies that have greeted Africans who have recently taken the treacherous trip across the Mediterranean to Spain, Italy, and Greece bring these ideas of modernity to the fore in terms of the global impact of unplanned migrations for the discourses and ideals of liberal democracies. The state policing of these migrants demonstrates quite clearly that liberal democracies are not fundamentally concerned with questions of freedom.

Let us take as an example the Dutch public intellectual, now based in the USA, Ayaan Hirsi Ali. Hirsi Ali has provided us with a rich archive with which to think these problems. Her collaborative film with Theo van Gogh, *Submission*, and her two books, *The Caged Virgin* and the autobiography *Infidel*, are well worth engaging. When one views and reads Hirsi Ali's work, one is struck by the seductiveness of modernity's ideals at the same time that it is clear that European modernity is only a partial human endeavor. I mean that it is only partially human in terms of its desire to fulfill all human potential. Hirsi Ali's impact has more to do with an easily recognizable trope of modernity — that of progression —

than with any specific insights she might offer to the threat that political Islam makes against the West. The narrative of progress is such a powerful and simultaneously commonsensical aspect of modernist discourse that it has become almost unmarked as a central tenet of the discourse. Hirsi Ali inhabits it fully, it is indeed her *raison d'être*.

I am interested in Hirsi Ali because, in Canada, the same narrative of progress that animates her critique underpins the Canadian debate on the idea of multiculturalism. It is not surprising, then, that the Grano Speakers Series and the Dominion Institute have celebrated her here. Hirsi Ali's critique mobilizes personal experience, as well as ideas of liberal democracy and its progressive narrative of freedoms through an engagement with questions of gender and religion, which translates well to the Canadian context. In fact, her argument on every count is that Islam is more fundamentalist than any other world religion. She writes in *Caged* that "there are Christians and Jews who raise their children in the belief that they are God's chosen people, but among Muslims the feeling that God has granted them special salvation goes further."[24] And she tells us that as she examined Islam, she came to realize a number of elements:

> The first of these is that a Muslim's relationship with his God is one of fear. A Muslim's conception of God is absolute. Our God demands total submission. He rewards you if you follow His

rules meticulously. He punishes you cruelly if you break His rules, both on earth, with illness and natural disasters, and in the hereafter, with hellfire.[25]

Hirsi Ali goes on to blame Islam's "backwardness" on tribal Arab history and values. Perhaps tellingly, the question of tribe and values also dominates the Canadian multiculturalism debate. Indeed, the question of tribe is central to my position. For what the post-colonial moment and the post-9/11 moment point to quite clearly is that the Euro-American tribe of whiteness is held together by an insistence that its view of the world is the only tenable view. That view has been instituted and perpetuated in coercive, violent, and non-coercive ways for over five hundred years. While many resistances have been mounted against its full institution, it has nonetheless triumphed in a fashion that exceeds its ongoing probability to maintain its hold and reach. Moreover, in moments of its potential demise, this tribal view has consistently been held together by all kinds of force. White anxiety works to bring into focus the networks necessary for holding the Euro-American tribal view of the world in place. The mounting articulation of different worldviews are mobilized as evidence that the Euro-American way is under siege. Thus, this white anxiety also comes with a great deal of white paranoia.

Conclusion: We are All Multicultural Still

In her assessment of the Rodney King verdict in

1992, Judith Butler articulated the notion of white paranoia to make sense of why the jury would acquit in the
case.[26] A similar condition is being expressed in the attacks
on multiculturalism as an idea. These attacks reflect a
desire to both hold on to the myth of Canada as a white
nation-state and to simultaneously racially manage the
necessary migrations for the perpetuation of late capitalism. Contrary to uncritical discourses which position
rationality as fundamental to Euro-American political
philosophy, white paranoia and anxiety operate in the
fault lines of racial mythologies of "superior" and "inferior." They further impose an order on their own irra-
tionality in terms of racial difference, while at the same
time grappling with certain kinds of economic rationali-
ties that complicate those ideational myths and practices.
Stein et al.'s disgraceful and intellectually dishonest debate
betrays the symptoms of white anxiety and paranoia not
merely with "an empire that strikes back" — to use a
phrase that helped to inaugurate the post-civil-rights,
post-colonial moment — but with an unruly empire that
is everywhere and thus needs management.

If, post-9/11, multiculturalism is now over, the
problems of racism, colonialism, and Europe's global
dominance remain firmly with us. On one hand, multiculturalism as state policy sought to put in place structures
to perpetuate various forms of dominance. On the other
hand, the idea of multiculturalism sought to produce
modes of being that might allow for a decolonial project
of freedom. State multiculturalism was only meant to be
a compromise on the way to producing different social

relations and thus producing forms of humanity that might be radically different from those that European coloniality has bequeathed us. Any debate that seeks to seriously engage the questions of multiculturalism must take seriously that the concept is deeply bound up in European global domination, which can only end if and when other ways of being are accorded the same conceptual and material expression as Europe's claims have been thus far.

Originally published in *Home and Native Land: Unsettling Multiculturalism in Canada.* Chazan, M., Helps, L., Stanley, A. and Thakkar, S. (ed.). Between the Lines: Toronto, 2011: 15-30.

Notes

1. From George Bush to Irshad Manji to Tarek Fatah, the idea that Western conceptions of freedom and democracy are the best way to live a life has been perpetuated
2. Morrison, *Playing in the Dark*, 37
3. Ibid., 38
4. Buck-Morss, "Hegel and Haiti," 821
5. Gilroy, *The Black Atlantic: Modernity and Double Consciousness*, 5
6. Buck-Morss, "Hegel and Haiti," 821
7. Both Trouillot and Fischer provide accounts of modernity, and particularly its discourses of freedom, which allow for understanding how deeply unfreedom is embedded in European emancipatory discourses. Their work helps us to make better sense of how post-Enlightenment ideas of freedom are founded on the denial of freedom to racialized and enslaved others who exposed Euro-American contradictions concerning freedom
8. Hall, "Universities, Intellectuals, and Multitudes," 123
9. Mills, *The Racial Contract*
10. Onstad, "Exploring Humanity, Violence and All,"
11. Ibid.
12. Gregg, "Identity Crisis," 38-47; Bliss, "Has Canada Failed?" 3-5; Janice Stein, "Living Better Multiculturally," 3-5; Foster, "Pierre Trudeau would have approved our new G-G," A13; "A regal statement about gender and race," A21
13. Ibbitson, "Canada's tolerance conundrum," A4; Sid-

diqui, "Charter, gender equity and freedom of religion," A21

14. Foster "Somewhere, Over the Rainbow," A17
15. David Scott, *Refashioning Futures*, 8
16. Janice Stein et al, *Uneasy Partners: Multiculturalism and Rights in Canada*.
17. Foster, *Where Race Does not Matter*, 120
18. Ibid.
19. Foster, *Blackness and Modernity*, 103-4
20. Hall, "Conclusion: the Multi-cultural Question," 209
21. Wynter, *Do Not Call Us Negros*, 31
22. Taylor, "Multiculturalism and the Politics of Recognition," 132
23. See the work of Angela Davis, Ruth Wilson Gilmore and Julia Sudbury as examples
24. Hirsi Ali, *The Caged Virgin*, x
25. Ibid., xi
26. Butler, "Endangered/Endangering: Schematic Racism and White Paranoia," 15-22

References

Bliss, Michael. "Has Canada Failed?" *Literary Review of Canada*, March 2006.

Buck-Morss, Susan. "Hegel and Haiti," *Critical Inquiry*, 26, no.4 (2000).

Butler, Judith. "Endangered/Endangering: Schematic Racism and White Paranoia," In *Reading Rodney King/ Reading Urban Uprising*, edited by Robert Gooding-Williams. New York: Routledge, 1993.

Foster, Cecil. "Pierre Trudeau would have approved our

new G- G," *The Globe and Mail*, August 5, 2005.

———. *Where Race Does not Matter: The New Spirit of Modernity*. Toronto: Penguin Canada, 2005.

———. "A regal statement about gender and race," *The Globe and Mail*, September 07, 2006.

———. "Somewhere, Over the Rainbow," *The Globe and Mail*, June 20, 2006.

———. *Blackness and Modernity: The Colour of Humanity and the Quest for Freedom*. Montreal and Kingston: McGill-Queens University Press, 2007.

Gilroy, Paul. *The Black Atlantic: Modernity and Double Consciousness*. Cambridge; Harvard University Press, 1993

Gregg, Allan. "Identity Crisis," *Walrus Magazine,* March, 2006.

Hall, Stuart. "Conclusion: the Multi-cultural Question," In *Un/settled Multiculturalisms: Diasporas, Entangle- ments, Transruptions,* edited by Barnor Hess, London: Zeb Books, 2006.

———. "Universities, Intellectuals, and Multitudes," In *Utopian Pedagogy: Radical Experiments against Neoliberal Globalization*, edited by Mark Coté, Richard Day & Greig de Peuter. Toronto: University of Toronto Press, 2007.

Hirsi Ali, Ayaan. *The Caged Virgin: An Emancipation Proclamation for Women and Islam*. New York: Free Press, 2006.

Ibbitson, John. "Canada's tolerance conundrum," *The Globe and Mail*, September 6, 2006.

Mills, Charles. *The Racial Contract*. Chicago: University of Chicago Press, 2007.

Morrison, Toni. *Playing in the Dark: Whiteness and the Literary Imagination* Cambridge: Harvard University Press, 1992.

Onstad, Katrina. "Exploring Humanity, Violence and All," *The New York Times*, September 16, 2007, http://www.ny- times.com/2007/09/16/movies/160 nst.html

Scott, David. *Refashioning Futures: Criticism after Post- coloniality.* Princeton, New Jersey: Princeton University Press, 1999.

Siddiqui, Haroon. "Charter, gender equity and freedom of re- ligion," *Toronto Star*, September 7, 2006.

Stein, Janice. "Living Better Multiculturally," *Literary Review of Canada*, September, 2006.

Stein, Janice. et al. *Uneasy Partners: Multiculturalism and Rights in Canada.* Waterloo: Wilfrid Laurier Press, 2007.

Taylor, Charles. "Multiculturalism and the Politics of Recognition," In *Multiculturalism*, edited by Amy Gutman. ed. Princeton, New Jersey: Princeton University Press, 1994.

Wynter, Sylvia. *Do Not Call Us Negros: How Multicultural Textbooks Perpetuate Racism.* San Francisco: Aspire Books, 1992.

Chapter 5

Spoken Word and Afrodiasporic Performances of Race Memory

This month marks the thirtieth anniversary of Bob Marley's death. Marley, the international Jamaican reggae superstar, embodies Black diaspora and African desires for post-1960s liberation. Marley's music and his actions worked to conjoin Africa and its diaspora in a chanting down of Babylon that was both anti-imperialist and simultaneously a critique of post-colonial disappointment. In short, Marley's music called for a new global revolution in which Africa and Afrodiasporic peoples would play a central role in reshaping the globe. In fact, it might be argued that Marley's music, especially, in songs such as "Redemption Song" and "War," positioned the liberation of Africa and Afrodiasporic peoples as the epicenter of global liberation and freedom in a post-60s world. His music was indeed a radical call for global revolution. In the aftermath of Marley's death, post-colonial disappointment is even more firmly evident in the geopolitics of the regions that his music most intimately spoke to.

However, this spring, revolution is in the air almost everywhere as we commemorate Marley's life and legacy. From the Middle East to North Africa, to Greece to Britain to even the USA (Wisconsin), the stirrings of revolution have arisen. In yet another moment of the deep crisis that capitalism repeatedly brings us, revolt and revolution appear to be on the horizon. Frantz Fanon, diagnosing the colonial economic condition and relation in the context of an emerging of anti-colonial movement, state, and condition, offers a stunning prophetic assessment of our present global times. He writes:

> It happens that few countries fulfill the conditions demanded by the trusts and monopolies. Thus capital, failing to find a safe outlet, remains blocked in Europe, and is frozen. It is all the more frozen because the capitalists refuse to invest in their countries. The returns in this case are in fact negligible and treasury control is the despair of even the boldest spirits.
>
> In the long run the situation is catastrophic. Capital no longer circulates, or else its circulation is considerably diminished. In spite of the huge sums swallowed up by military budgets, international capitalism is in desperate straits.[1]

The kinds of crises that are currently confronting Greece, Spain, and a European city near you soon are echoed in Fanon's insights. And clearly a significant element of the Middle Eastern and North American uprisings are central to Fanon's diagnosis of how colonial and now post-colonial capital circulates, freezes, and produces despair. Fanon continues further in his critique of colonial capital hegemony and the role that the colonized and now formerly colonized will play in global liberation by articulating a potential "new humanism." He writes:

> They will not manage to divide the progressive forces which mean to lead mankind towards happiness by brandishing the threat of a Third World which is rising like the tide to swallow up Europe … What it expects from those who for centuries have kept it in slavery is that they will help it to rehabilitate mankind, and make man victorious everywhere, once and for all … This huge task which consists of reintroducing mankind into the world, the whole of mankind, will be carried out with the indispensable help of European peoples, who themselves must realize that in the past they have often joined the ranks of our common masters where colonial questions are concerned. To achieve this, the European peoples must first decide to wake up and shake themselves, use their brains, and stop playing the stupid game of the Sleeping Beauty.[2]

Or put another way by Bob Marley, in "War":

Until the philosophy which hold one race
superior
And another
Inferior
Is finally

And permanently
Discredited
And abandoned—
Everywhere is war —
Me say war.

That until there are no longer
First-class and second-class citizens of any
nation
Until the color of a man's skin
Is of no more significance than the colour of
his eyes —
Me say war.

That until the basic human rights
Are equally guaranteed to all,
Without regard to race —
Dis a war.

That until that day
The dream of lasting peace,
World citizenship
Rule of international morality
Will remain in but a fleeting illusion to be
pursued,
But never attained —
Now everywhere is war — war.[3]

Those two radical reorderings of the globe announced
by Fanon in the opening pages of *Wretched of the Earth* and

by Marley in "War" articulate revolt, revolution, and transformative global human change. These two Antilleans offer us a global reading and accounting for which the only term useful to describing their perspective is revolution — continuous revolution. "Revolution" is a word both bandied about much and simultaneously hated, especially in a post-Marxist, post-Bolshevik world.

In contemporary culture, the word "revolution" is often used to mark significant cultural changes outside of the political realm; for example, each time the technology industries release a new product for personal consumption, it is greeted as some kind of revolution. On the other hand, revolution as political change and transformation is often downplayed in our present historical moment, especially when it is anti-capitalist and/ or decolonial. The ways in which the term "revolution" is deployed are crucial for the arguments I wish to make in this paper, because I intend to suggest that Afrodiasporic performance artists, through a range of engagements with pressing political, social, and cultural issues, have kept alive the possibilities of revolt and revolution, as their words/art revolts against normative understandings of current global arrangements. In so doing, they have kept alive a notion of revolution as embedded in human possibilities and thus in the remaking of the genres of the human, as Sylvia Wynter would put it. The artists I will discuss below work across economy, politics, culture, race, and sexuality to revolt against the current global hegemony that would have us believe that global revolt is not possible, but, importantly, these artists provide us accounts of contemporary arrangements that require us to think what the opposite of a lack of revolting might mean for humankind. In short, these artists ask that we consider nothing less than revolution.

Raymond Williams, in his definition of revolution in *Keywords*, reminds us that prior to "revolution" making it into the English language, the only words useful for describing the kind of change that revolution can signal were "treason" and "rebellion." "Treason" carried with it a sense of betraying lawful authority, and "rebellion" was mostly understood as armed uprising and renewal through violence. Williams points out that in the English language, "revolution" moved from a circular understanding to an understanding of uprising and violent change. Williams' definition is in keeping with Julia Kristeva's articulation that "revolt," the close relative of revolution, "first implies the notion of movement, the second, that of space and time."[3] In *The Sense and Non-sense of Revolt*, Kristeva is interested in a culture of revolt, and she suggests "an urgent need to develop the culture of revolt starting with our aesthetic heritage and find new variants of it,"[4] of which I would argue that Bob Marley's "rebel music" and its descendent, Afrodiasporic spoken word are important elements of such aesthetic heritage. Kristeva puts ideas of psychoanalysis into conversation with the social to make a case for why revolt is crucial to the survival of our culture. She writes: "When the excluded have no culture of revolt and must content themselves with regressive ideologies, with shows and entertainments that far from satisfy the demand of pleasure, they become rioters."[5] This point of Kristeva's is one I shall return to below. What distinguishes a revolution from a riot is important to note.

The language of revolution has been central to spoken word and dub poetry since its inception. Whether one is thinking of the work of early poets like Mutabaruka, Linton Kwesi Johnson, Benjamin Zephaniah, Lillian Allen, and Mikey Smith, the idea of revolt and revolution has been a cornerstone of both the aesthetics and political desires of dub poetry, as well as central to its form. The originators of the form forged music and poetry with biting political commentary to produce a popular art form that is committed to revolt in both style and substance. Revolt occurs first in the use of language, the resistance to the page, the insistence on the oral and the deliberate paring of words to both undermine normalcy and highlight modes of governance, which benefit the minority at the expense of the majority. Thus, as suggested earlier, this art form, which takes as its foundation the rebel music of reggae, remains committed to imagining a different kind of future. If in the first instance spoken word and dub poetry performance was concerned with the biting commentary of post-colonial disappointment, then its more contemporary incarnations cast its poetic nets much further to articulate a post-colonial disappointment that is not merely about national disappointment and global coloniality — even though those ideas remain central. Contemporary poetics takes up questions of global terror, racist nationalisms, gender, and sexuality as ways of extending and critiquing the hetero-patriarchal state and contemporary politics. Central to all of those concerns is an insistent critique of global capitalism, in short the call for a revolution in human relations as currently organized.

Spoken word as a performative political possibility dwells in what Kamau Brathwaite in "Middle Passages: a Lecture" calls the literature of catastrophe. This literature of catastrophe as he understands it takes its most potent insights from the severe reordering of the globe since the fall of the Roman Empire but reaches a nadir during transatlantic slavery, plantation slavery in the Americas, aboriginal land theft, genocide and near genocide, and the invention of a form of capitalism that orders all of life today. The literature of catastrophe, then, marks a global epoch in which Europe instates and dictates a way of seeing and living as the only possible way to be human. Such practices produced catastrophic results for many others. Spoken word artists speak into, not just about, the ongoing lingering effects and affects of such global catastrophe; it is the source of spoken word's performative uprising. Brathwaite, drawing on his "tidelectical" analysis of the situation, argues that the literature of catastrophe should result in a carnivalization of the West. Such a carnivalization is both Bahktinian and slave-derived, moving towards revolution if not outright revolution. Central to the unfolding catastrophe that Brathwaite maps for us is the question of the production of unfreedom for many.

Hannah Arendt, writing in the aftermath of other

moments of the catastrophic production of unfreedom, the Shoah and totalitarianism, turns to revolution to makes sense of the frames through which human possibility might be achieved. She is indeed concerned with the question of freedom.

> Crucial, then, to any understanding of revolution in the modern age is that the idea of freedom and the existence of a new beginning should coincide. And since the current notion of the Free World is that freedom, and neither justice nor greatness, is the highest criterion for judging the constitutions of political bodies, it is not only our understanding of revolution but our conception of freedom, clearly revolutionary in origin, on which may hinge the extent to which we are prepared to accept or reject this coincidence.[6]

The centrality of ideas of freedom to revolution cannot be underestimated. To reduce revolution down to only the economic and the social misses a significant component of why people sacrifice themselves for its possibility. Freedom, then, is something that must be humanly made and protected. As Arendt writes, freedom is "the product of human effort and qualities of the man-made world."[7] Therefore, how freedom and its desires are articulated is crucial to how revolt and revolution can happen.

Before I continue my argument about revolution — and I am optimistic that we are in the clutches of potential global revolt and revolution, though it might be a long one with many starts and stops — I want to turn to some examples of how the idea of freedom is kept alive in spoken word performativity as a mode of desired being and as a force against normalization. In Staceyann Chin's "Feminist or a Womanist," she does not restage the conversation between Euro-American feminism and African-American womanism as two opposing ideological and political practices based on a woman's point of view of the world. Instead, she offers an accounting of the world in which women's insights might allow us to see it much more clearly. In her poetic quest for freedom, she engages nationalism, gender, ethnicity, and sexuality, and even the minutia of campus politics is unhinged and put back together again as a mode of life. The work points to the matrix that prohibits freedom's possibilities and calls for their undoing. The poem's language enacts the desires for freedom, and if such desires were unleashed, we would be on the cusp of revolution — a reordering of the genre of the human as we presently know it and live it.

Or take as another example "Oh Canada," Boonaa Mohammed's rewriting of the Canadian national anthem in a post-9/11 world. Boonaa's intervention does not merely recite the history of Canada as a colonial space of conquest, but also seeks to put that history into play as the foundation for post-9/11 practices of detention, surveillance, and various forms of profiling. The accumulated effect of Boonaa's inventory is the unleashing of a different mode and idea of freedom than that which all the violations of the human are subjected to in a post-9/11 world under the rhetoric of freedom and democracy. Boonaa's intervention, then, does not only recall and remind, it also seeks to set in play the desires for transformative change. Writing about similar performative strategies in the 1990s,[8] I have previously argued that what such performances do is demonstrate the Janus-face of the nation and point to the ways in which nations produce imaginary regimes of belonging. If ideas of multiculturalism were meant to suture previous unimagined members into the nation, then its post-9/11 attacks (by no less than German chancellor Angela Merkel and British prime minister David Cameron in recent declarations about the failure of multiculturalism) speak to not merely its failure to do so but also to its failure to adequately account for the histories that brought us into this catastrophic encounter — that is, it failed to account for the world we presently have and the past that got us here. Boonaa Mohammed is enacting multiculturalism's alter-ego, if you will.

Maria Caridad Casas, writing about more formal poetry, is keenly aware of the tension between the page and spoken word. In Casas' work, the question of language as a sign and a signal is highlighted. Following scholars of semiotics, Casas understand Caribbean-Canadian poetics as a form of multimodality. Casas' work focuses on the language techniques that move from the oral to the page and then the oral again in Black Canadian (Caribbean) feminist poetics. Her work is concerned with thinking through the politics and the social as they are represented and presented in a poetics that is much concerned with the idea of revolt as it attempts to represent revolt on the page and in its sound/song. Spoken word is, then, deeply influenced by the creole conditions produced out of the catastrophic encounters unleashed in a post-Columbus globe. Contemporary spoken word and dub poetry is therefore a highly symbolic production of the global creole "underclass." In such circumstances, the social and the political rear their heads as the source for potential revolution. What, following Casas, we might call the struggle with language is indicative of the larger struggles that frame our historical and contemporary lives. In a summative moment about the poets she studies, that I believe extends to spoken word, Casas makes this claim: "Although still written, their poetry is oral; if oral, then also embodied, then also participating in discourses of race, gender, sexuality, and a host of other systems of social organization and individual identity."[9]

Let me then return to our present revolutionary time and the place of spoken word performativity in it. Spoken word and dub poetry are immediate forms, sometimes even improvisational. Much like revolutions, spoken word is constituted out of a sense of the people, even though unlike revolutions the singularity of the poet and their work remains the central force. What is often not commented on in the celebratory moments that announce Facebook and Twitter revolutions is the manner in which the technology is being utilized in a form reminiscent of orality and simultaneously the *longue durée* that has built up to these revolutions to make them more than uprisings. The quest for freedom in these revolutions is mostly articulated by their leaderless revolt and lack of a recognizable political agenda outside the language of freedom. It is in such fashion that I put spoken word as a form in the social lexicon of movement towards revolution, or put differently, spoken word artists have been insistent on the possibility of revolution, and they have kept its possibilities in the zeitgeist as a significant desire for a different human future. Arendt, in the conclusion of *On Revolution*, also turns to poets to make her case concerning how the new spirit of revolution failed to find the necessary institutions that might sustain them:

> There is nothing that could compensate for this failure or prevent it from becoming final, except memory and recollection. And since the storehouse of memory is kept and watched over by the poets, whose business it is to find and make the words we live by ... in order to find an approximate articulation of the actual content of our lost treasure.[10]

Arendt concludes her study with two poets. Chet Singh's *Recessionary Revolutionaries* speaks both to the immediacy of spoken word and dub poetry and to the question of how the poet represents our failed present and potential libratory future. The title track from the album/collection takes as its stance the neo-liberal "revolution" as it has normalized life, and so impeded actual revolution.

What I have elsewhere referred to as neoliberal culture, in an attempt to make the case that all of the factors of neoliberal economics now organize human life — surveillance, audits, managerialism, and so on — is central to the accounting that Singh offers in his poem. On the entire album, Singh is interested in both the micro and macro orientations of neoliberal structures as those structures prevent and prohibit modes of being human that could radically transform our globe. Coming after the 2008 global capitalist meltdown, Singh's words remind us that everywhere people resist they are arrested — he thus chants "culture has been arrested." The significant call, then, is for a peoples' revolt that will unlock culture and write a new story of our times. What is particularly crucial about spoken word and dub poetry in this moment is its universalism from below perspective, a perspective that draws those now made into *homo economicus* into a global block requiring and demanding different kinds of human lives. Singh's *Recessionary Revolutionaries* articulates such desires in its nine tracks that range from radical politics to the environment to global recession and calls to act against neoliberalism's global order.

In conclusion, I have deliberately focused on form as opposed to identity as a way to make my claims about freedom, since freedom is non-identarian. Bob Marley's continuing global impression is about more than his image, despite the attempt to render him only that. His appeal continues to be in the mode of articulating freedom's potential, for which thirty years after his death his music remains a global soundtrack. Let us return to Fanon, then, one last time:

> The colonized man who writes for his people
> ought to use the past with the intention of open-
> ing the future, as an invitation to action and a
> basis for hope. But to ensure that hope and to
> give it form, he must take part in action and
> throw himself body and soul into the national
> struggle.[11]

I would bravely amend Fanon only to assert that in our moment this is global struggle. Capitalism's permanent crises are being managed through modes of difference in which a second middle passage from Africa to Europe has firmly announced itself; this time it seeks to put into relation the evidences, as in bodies and lives, of the catastrophic reorderings of post-Columbus movements. Our "new" global intimacy requires increasing forms of violence to hold such intimacy at bay, all the while celebrating an anemic global traffic of capital and its elite defenders. Revolution means to topple this and is on its way to doing so.

The remaking of mankind or genres of the human, as Fanon and Wynter respectively term what is at stake, in a reordering of the globe in which freedom is possible, requires us to grapple with the "race memory" of enlightenment and modernity time and again, as not just belonging to non-white people but as the foundation of a range of practices and ideas that have come to organize all of human life. The phrase "race memory" in my title is meant to invoke what Hannah Arendt might call universal responsibility. Arendt writes: "For the idea of humanity, when purged of all sentimentality, has the very serious consequence that in one form or another men must assume responsibility for all crimes committed by men and that all nations share the onus of evil committed by others."[12] Arendt might appear to be offering a one-size-fits-all model, but I think something else is at stake in her suggestion. An ethical accounting is at stake. It is one in which the mathematics of human-ness requires a radical recalculation in which only revolution, this time global revolution, can produce the space and time of freedoms we have not yet achieved. Spoken word artists and dub poets keep us listening for the signs of revolt.

Originally published in *AfroFictional In[Ter]Ventions: Revisiting The BIGSAS Festival of African* (-Diasporic) Literatures, Bayreuth 2011-2013. S. Arndt and N. Ofuatey-Alazard (Ed.). Edition Assemblage: Munster, 2014, p. 59-66.

Notes:

1. Fanon, *The Wretched of the Earth*, 104
2. Ibid., 106
3. Williams, *Keywords*, 1
4. Kristeva, *The Sense and Non-sense of Revolt*, 7
5. Ibid.
6. Arendt, *The Human Condition*,19
7. Ibid., 21
8. Walcott, *Black Like Who*

9. Casas, *Multimodality in Canadian Black Feminist Writing*, 160
10. Arendt, *On Revolution*, 272
11. Fanon, *The Wretched of the Earth*, 232
12. Arendt, *Essays in Understanding*, 131

References

Arendt, Hannah. *The Human Condition*. Chicago: University of Chicago Press, 1958.

———. *Essays in Understanding 1930-1954: Formation, Exile, and Totalitarianism*. New York: Schocken Books, 1994.

———. *On Revolution*. New York: Penguin Classics, 2006.

Brathwaite, Kamau. "Middle Passages: A Lecture." Canada: Sandberry Press, 2006.

Casas, Maria Caridad. *Multimodality in Canadian Black Feminist Writing: Orality and the Body in the Work of Harris, Phillip, Allen, and Brand*. Amsterdam: Rodopi, 2009.

Fanon, Frantz. *Wretched of the Earth*. New York: Grove Press, Inc., 1963.

Kristeva, Julia. *The Sense and Non-sense of Revolt*, translated by Jeanine Herman. New York: Columbia University Press, 2000.

Walcott, Rinaldo. *Black Like Who: Writing Black Canada*. Toronto: Insomniac Press, 1997.

Williams, Raymond. *Keywords*. London: Fontana Press, 1988.

Chapter 6

Queer Returns: Human Rights, the Anglo-Caribbean, and Diaspora Politics

This history breeds the need for activating an ethical imperative atrophied by gradual distancing from the narrative of — progress colonialism/capitalism. This is the argument about cultural suturing, learning from below to supplement with the possibility of the subjectship of rights.[1]

Introduction: A life in-between position

In the spring of 2008, Thomas Glave published the anthology *Our Caribbean: A Gathering of Lesbian and Gay Writing from the Antilles*. The book has been greeted with a great deal of enthusiasm, and rightly so; its reception has been hailed as a singularly important moment in the politics and debates of Caribbean non-heterosexual identities and practices. Glave has been meticulous in documenting the responses to the book, which reportedly took him about six years to compile, with some works translated into English for the first time. *Our Caribbean* is a pan-Caribbean anthology; most of the languages of the region are represented in the book, and it consists of prose fiction alongside critical essays as well as personal essays. For full disclosure, I contributed an essay to the anthology.[2]

All authors are given a nation-state designation in the book even if they have not resided in that nation-state for most of their life (for example, Dionne Brand, Trinidad; Makeda Silvera, Jamaica; while some authors are given two or three designations, which seem to be based on the geo-political territory their writing covers, but also hints at nation-state belonging: Walcott, Barbados/Canada; Audre Lorde, Grenada/Barbados/USA, and therein lies the first set of basic difficulties with the work of such an anthology. How does such an anthology negotiate diaspora and in particular second-order diasporas? Despite such difficulties, difficulties that I consider significant even if basic, reviewers have generally glowed about the anthology, mostly seeing it as a very important "coming out party" for Caribbean queers. The book is read as an important plank in the struggle for rights in the region.

For example, Dr. Cathie Koa Dunsford wrote a glowing review of the anthology, calling it must-read material and urging colleagues to take it up as a course text.[3] Most importantly, she understands the anthology as taking up Audre Lorde's work and project and extending it into our present conditions of human existence. Dunsford's review champions the anthology as a subaltern truth-telling that brings to the table voices of those not often heard and sometimes never heard. Her one caution is that the anthology would have benefited from more local regional voices — that is, voices in place in the region currently — and fewer "expats;" in other words, the anthology suffers from the usual problem of those in the diaspora speaking back to "home." Dunsford's claim points back to the difficulty of how second-order diasporas are placed in such conversations and relations. But still she reminds us that the anthology now sets in place an important foundation for those still living in the region to build on. A kind of developmental model is immediately present in her comments, and yet her comments also point to the difficult politics and ethics of the undertaking tackled by Glave. In other shorter and less nuanced reviews, the developmental model is explicitly clearer.[4] It is the twin problematics of ideas of development and its metaphors and the ethics of queer returns "home" that I try to probe in this essay. I want to suggest that my argument is more complex and complicated than who gets to speak and especially what they get to say.

Thomas Glave has emerged as an important figure in Anglo-Caribbean queer organizing and politics. He quietly helped to found J-FLAG (Jamaican Forum of Lesbians, All-Sexuals and Gays) and then published a quite trenchant and daring letter calling out Jamaica on its nationally instituted homo-hatred ("Toward a Nobility of the Imagination: Jamaica's Shame [An Open Letter to the People of Jamaica]").[5] More recently, he has again challenged the prime minister of Jamaica, Bruce Golding, on homophobic comments made in Britain (Calabash Literary Festival, May 27, 2008). Glave cuts an interesting and arresting figure — a soft-spoken, dreadlock-wearing artist/intellectual who would easily pass as the embodiment of the stereotypical hypersexual Rasta man, were he not gay. But important for my purposes here, Glave is also a second-order diasporic figure — born in the USA of Jamaican parents and having lived in Jamaica and the USA, he travels between both and mostly seems to claim a Jamaican identity (Jamerican). I have spent this brief time on Glave as a form of personal analytical distancing in an attempt to think through the working of diasporic ethics and the claims of those belonging to the diaspora to participate in "home" affairs. I see my own ambivalent participation as similar to, if much more limited and circumscribed than, Glave's and many others' deep involvement in the region. It is at the moment of participation and the types and modes of participation that something crucial happens to how place, identity, politics, and ethics are constituted, played out, and positioned or articulated.

My own forays into working around queer sexual politics have proved equally troubling, perplexing, and complicated. For example, recent involvement with the Stop Murder Music Campaign (Canada) serves as a backdrop to both participating in activism surrounding the region and simultaneously challenging North American queer racism that seeks to imagine both the invisibility of Black gays and lesbians and our incapability of speaking and acting in our own interests.[6] But even with a campaign like Stop Murder Music one finds oneself inhabiting a Caribbean authenticity that might or might not be legitimate depending upon the various contexts in whch one might invoke a sense of Caribbean-ness to substantiate one's speech and actions. I thus speak as an ambivalent "extension" of the Anglo-Caribbean collectivity conditioned by a diasporic experience in North America positioned between resisting racism, homo-hatred, and white homonormative racism on the one hand and attempting to frame lives beyond those dynamics on the other. And in this regard, I speak as one among others whose practices, desires, and politics inform my own. Yet, I want to acknowledge the tripwires of speaking from here to there and to sound out what a possible ethics of speech when sounding off might sound like.

This essay, then, is informed by a particular politics of representation that moves beyond studies of representation of identity to query the representation of arguments and claims made on and in behalf of subordinated identities, in this case queer Anglo-Caribbean identities. Insofar as I query the claims of rights being made on behalf of Anglo-Caribbean queer identities, I also attempt to point to the trouble of speaking as a Caribbean person not living in the region and simultaneously to the ways in which my speech and thus my queries are informed by a politics of speaking back to white queer homonormativity in North America. This essay lies somewhere between the claim to speak in concert with Caribbean queers both in and out of the region and with Black North American queers who must refuse the idea and/or notion that we are in need of queer development from white queers. Put another way, this essay is about the ways in which ideas, in particular my own, are caught between white queer homonormative racism and Anglo-Caribbean homo-hatred, at the same time that I attempt to offer a critique of rights discourse. In short, this is tricky but necessary business if progressive political struggles seek to do more than produce proliferations of identities and instead work towards the production of nation-states where life is livable on terms that produce human-ness in all its complicated diversities without state judgment and/or sanction.

In this essay, then, I move from North America to the Anglo-Caribbean and back to North America as an indication of the ways in which both the experience of diaspora and an ethics of diaspora might provide a space from which to speak and make a politics present and/or appear. In this regard, I draw on the queer ideas of Édouard Glissant to articulate what I call "homopoetics." This homopoetics allows me to read across various spaces and texts and to make some truth claims. More specifically, homopoetics allows me to draw on regional and diasporic flows to engage discourses of homophobia and "rights talk" as those discourses and ideas circulate in different sites, building a narrative of the queer Caribbean and a homophobic Caribbean simultaneously.

Further, I am influenced by the work of Sara Ahmed's *Queer Phenomenology: Orientations, Objects, Others*, in which she writes the following: "Now in living a queer life, the act of going home, or going back to the place I was brought up, has a certain disorienting effect."[7] Her insights on phenomenological experiences in terms of queer orientations help me to problematize how returns home inform my practices and politics of queerness in the diaspora. Significantly, this work is about how a queer diasporic Anglo-Caribbean might speak to the project of "rights talk" and homophobia, as a displaced subject backwards and forwards, in and out of the region. Put another way, this essay is in part concerned with the ethical responsibilities and dilemmas of diaspora subjects as subjects who also speak back to somewhere from another and certain place. Like Ahmed, this speaking back for me is disorienting, but simultaneously it is an ethical orientation of what a diaspora subjecthood, location, and position might contribute to a politics of the possible and the future — dilemmas notwithstanding. The privilege of being a North American queer who can claim the region, speak within it and with it, and remain on the edge of it poses an ethical dilemma in the face of numerous political desires, especially when one questions the limits of rights.

Queer returns

Since the eruptions around dancehall signaled by Buju Banton's "Boom Bye Bye" in the 1990s (1993 to be exact), the Anglo-Caribbean has been cast as one of the most homophobic places in the world — with Jamaica as its epicenter. In the midst of this homophobia, Anglo-Caribbean queers have found themselves the objects of rescue fantasies, both real and imagined, around the Western world.[8] Between the vulgar homophobia of verbal harassment and actual death in Jamaica, and the milder ridicule in other places of the region, which requires queerness to always appear queer and/or act out of the ordinary, thus affirming heterosexual as ordinary, a certain kind of urgency for activating a queer politics and movement is now present. But that present also has a past.

I have written elsewhere, in concert with Kobena Mercer's claim that "sexual politics is the Achilles heel of Black liberation,"[9] that Fanon's claim of no homosexuality in the Antilles opens up possibilities for thought on the subject.[10] Mercer's insight is an attempt to wrestle with Fanon's claim of the absence of homosexuality in the Antilles, as Fanon is positioned in the politics and narratives of Black liberation struggles. My rejoinder in concert with Mercer is, at the least, to point to how Fanon notices homosexuality among Antilleans in Paris and attempts to think it originates there. So if no homosexuality exists in the Antilles, then it can still be acquired when movement or travel happens. Such an acquisition does not make the acts of homosexuality and being Antillean any less valid. But what it does open up is what can and must be accounted for once the status is seen or acknowledged. Fanon finds and is able to recognize homosexual Antilleans in Paris; he knows the signs of homosexuality if only we are to believe that he learned them only in France. But he already undermines such generosity by alerting us to, at the least, gender trouble coded as potential non-heterosexuality that he terms "godmothers" in his famous footnote number 21.[11] Were we to read Fanon in ahistorical terms, his comments open up the possibility for second-order diasporas to be the authoritative speakers on Caribbean homosexuality since it is acquired abroad. However, there is much evidence to prove Fanon faulty in his thinking on this topic. What Fanon does not consider in his footnote are the modes of suppression (heteronormativity) and the modes of expression ("men dressed like women") in defining or at least marking homosexuality in and out of the Antilles.

Moving to Caribbean extensions or diaspora by another name, in Hilton Als' memoir, *The Women,* he offers a richer interior perspective of the ways in which some Caribbean people approach non-heterosexual expressivity. He writes: "Being an auntie man enamored of Negressity is all I have ever known to be."[12] He further states: "I have expressed my Negressity by living, fully, the prescribed life of an auntie man — what Barbadians call a faggot."[13] Als writes into being his queerness as an expression of his Barbadian family's circumstances in 1970s New York. Concerning his mother, he writes:

> She had one friend who was an auntie man. Unlike other women who knew him as well, my mother didn't find her friend's sexual predilection confusing or anger-provoking. Besides, auntie men were not mysterious beings to her; in Barbados, most ostensibly straight men had sex with them, which was good, since that left women alone for a while. During the course of her friendship with Grantly the auntie man, she focused on him. Had she had access to other people besides her children, lover, employer, doctors, she might have been a fag hag, fond of auntie men, music, movies.[14]

The auntie man occupies a very specific place and function as long as his masculinity is recognizable as a specific type of "queer" masculinity. Als recalls the insult of "faggot" in his family as a disciplinary practice or what Sylvia Wynter calls "behavior orienting practices"[15] to keep him in line as a product of contradictory and ambivalent forces in Barbadian and Caribbean social relations, in particular the disciplinary control of matrilineal family structures and the fear of women not adequately raising boy children to be "real men." The insult in this case is a disciplinary orienting reminder of normative manliness. Importantly, too, Als' work calls to mind how the Anglo-Caribbean travels and how it hybridizes and changes in different spaces, even when specific and recognizable insults continue. The work of the insult is crucial to understanding some of the claims about Anglo-Caribbean homophobia, I would assert.

Extending the above view, in *Insult and the Making of the Gay Self*, Didier Eribon suggests that insults work to constitute queer community. His insight is premised on a reading of the insult that is both internal and external to queer communities. Eribon points out that one subset of insults is caricature in its many forms. As Eribon concedes, and I think that he is correct in his assertion, "gay identity is always forced to remember its origins in insult,"[16] which means that queers are never able to leave the insult behind. I would argue that what contemporary "rights talk" desires is to leave the insult behind, but the insult as function and practice might be the orienting device that queers require to turn identification into community. The work of the insult, then, separates and disciplines, but it is also community constituting. Thus, the work of the insult can also be orienting, to recall Ahmed.

Let us turn to Wesley Crichlow for another orienting moment. In his essay "History, (Re)Memory, Testimony and Biomythography," he in part charts his personal history of coming to terms with being a "buller man." With a nod to Audre Lorde and her use of "Zami," Crichlow details the double-edgedness of reclaiming buller man as culturally specific to tell a story of pain and humiliation;[17] his use of the term, by speaking to the ways it is an insult or meant to humiliate, is at the same time powerful as he claims it to render himself a powerful speaking subject in Caribbean culturally specific and historical terms — a powerful act of self-naming. What is useful about Crichlow's insights is the way in which across a range of social, cultural, and institutional practices he plots, in a manner similar to Als, the attempts to make a Caribbean masculinity that is counter to anything that the "buller man" might represent. The type of hegemonic heterosexual masculinity that Crichlow details makes the visibility of the assumed buller man's presence in the culture clear and present as its other. But that Crichlow is able to mobilize and use against its intent (an intent to harm) the buller man to critically engage Anglo-Caribbean culture is in part Eribon's claim above.

Without suggesting an apology for homophobia in the Caribbean and its extensions — there exist places in the European West where queer theory and queer bodies meet hostility, even if there is a sense of gay and lesbian "rights talk" put into play in the governmental sphere at the level of the state. I return to Didier Eribon, who writes as follows:

> In 1995, the year of the first enormous French Gay Pride, editorials in the press, from the right and the left, gave free reign to sentiments that can only be qualified as phobic. Gay Pride, they said, was a danger to democracy; the homosexual "separatism" that such events revealed threatened to "destroy the architecture of the nation," ... Newspapers went on to ... insult the field of lesbian and gay studies, which apparently represented a danger to knowledge, to culture, to thought, and to the university. [18]

Eribon's chronicling of such French responses to mass public expressions of homosexuality in the public sphere is, I repeat, not an excuse for the Caribbean. It is rather a challenge for all of us to think differently about the question of state institutions and "rights talk" for queers. Yet there are no rescue missions launched in and on behalf of French queer development from the rights-loving West.

For me, then, insult is an opening to a conversation of sorts in the Anglo-Caribbean and its extensions. The insult is, as some Bajans put it, a refusal to utter or say the word "homosexual," which works to help to produce a kind of queer subjecthood. Some men and women in

Barbados are thus said to be "that way" or "so." In the poetics of such speech acts is an opening up of a poetics of language, of talk, and of thought and thus the origins of a homopoetics rooted in the queer modernities of the Caribbean region. Furthermore, such unspeakability is in part the acknowledgement of a presence, and a presence that is understood as occupying a place among other kinds of presences, even if not spoken as such. To be "so" or "that way" is to be poetically called into existence — ambivalent though it may be.

Homopoetics: Lives in-between

The work of diaspora and/or Caribbean extensions outside the archipelago and the ethics of speaking from "away" can draw on the poetics of the region to speak back in ways that ethically inform a politics of the possible there and here. In *Caribbean Discourse*, Édouard Glissant writes the following: "I define as a free or natural poetics any collective yearning for expression that is not opposed to itself either at the level of what it wishes to express or at the level of the language that it puts into practice."[19] Glissant begins to formulate a notion of poetics that I find useful for beginning the work of formulating a Black diasporic homopoetics within the Americas. I am interested in the ways in which theories and studies of queerness, discourses of sexuality — especially gay, lesbian, and bi-sexual — work within Afro-American society to constitute conversations that work at the level of the ephemeral so as to produce communities of sharing and political identifications across a range of local, national, and international boundaries of desire and sex.

I am thus similarly interested in the bodies that circulate across and within the Atlantic and Caribbean zones of the Americas and the places and spaces those bodies occupy — imaginary and otherwise. I am interested in how these circulations get recast as rights talk and what might be at stake in such recastings. This interest in thinking the Black homosexual of the Americas, or what I will call "the homopoetics of relation," is particularly urgent and sensitive as HIV/AIDS comes to be a significant defining feature of the region of the Americas we call the Caribbean, simultaneously alongside the global claim of the region's exaggerated homophobia, as exemplified by Jamaican dancehall's global reach. At the same time, this homopoetics is concerned with the relation and non-relation between the epidemic of HIV/AIDS among African-Americans, its devastating impact on the African continent, and its increasing impact among Black Canadians and African-Canadians. In other words, Africa's diaspora and the imagined homeland are both at stake. Glissant is interested in movement, and I am too. I do not seek to queer Glissant; instead, I work with Glissant's rather queer theories and insistences to make links, if also ephemeral, concerning the relation or non-relation of thought as an exercise in making the political appear.

Specifically, Glissant claims two kinds of poetics: natural and forced. He proceeds to more fully define natural poetics as follows:

Even if the destiny of a community should be a miserable one, or its existence threatened, these poetics are the direct result of activity within the social body. The most daring or the most artificial experiences, the most radical questioning of self-expression, extend, reform, clash with a given poetics. This is because there is no incompatibility here between desire and expression. The most violent challenge to an established order can emerge from a natural poetics, when there is continuity between the challenged order and the disorder it negates.[20]

Glissant offers in his articulation of a natural or free poetics a method for "reading" and debate that might be useful for thinking blackness, queerness, and claims of homophobia within and across Black diasporic communities in the Americas. His natural poetics is an orienting device of sorts. It is a method of movement, it is a method of relation, and it is a method of thought. The movement is not merely one of bodies but ideas as well. The relation is not merely one of identity, it is politics, and it is ethics. The thought is not merely one of ideas and speech acts, but it is a queer insistence or, as Glissant puts it in another sense, it is a "that that" (*Poetics of Relation*) — which means it is an incitement to discourse.

The archipelago of the Caribbean is not merely a geographic space, but the Caribbean as an entity also extends beyond its geography as a global reality — it is an extension in time and space, into other places and spaces. For those of us who have any relation to the region (and that is all of us in the post-colonial modern world), which Sylvia Wynter has called "the archipelago of poverty," commitments can be complex and contradictory.[21] Significantly for those of us who are non-heterosexual, those commitments and identifications pose difficult dilemmas concerning political expression and demands, cultural desires and identifications, and relationships between place, nation, and space — especially in the extensions.

For example, Jacqui Alexander, a long-time commentator on questions of Caribbean sexuality and the state, best articulates the relation of place, space, politics, expression, and placement from or in a Caribbean extension. She writes in the essay "Erotic Autonomy as a Politics of Decolonization: Feminism, Tourism, and the State in the Bahamas":

> I write as an outsider, neither Bahamian national nor citizen and thus outside the repressive reach of the Bahamian state, recognizing that the consequences of being disloyal to heterosexuality fall differently on my body than on the bodies of those criminalized lesbians in the Bahamas for whom the state has foreclosed any public expression of community … I write as an outlaw in my own country of birth …[22]

The sentiment that Alexander so cogently articulates is one that begs for an interstitial analysis, an analysis of the between and the afar, one of movement. Alexander admits that she writes in the company of a regional and global feminist movement and political formation of which Bahamian and Caribbean women are a part. This claim of Alexander's is an important one because it pushes beyond the boundaries of the nation-state and more specifically the state, to bring into sight different political formations as it simultaneously confronts the state's management and criminalization of certain sexual practices. It is from the between and the afar that Relation is possible and that a homopoetics might be uttered. Diaspora furnishes one aspect of the structure of Relation as a moment of the afar that enables the political speech act of homopoetics that might bring us near or into Relation.

Poetics of Relation, Glissant claims, is an extension of *Caribbean Discourse*, "a reconstituted echo or a spiral retelling."[23] I read both texts as the impossible, unspeakable spoken of the creole Americas. The impossibility of speaking the creole Americas is more about US regional imperial hegemony than it is about either a conceptual claim or an empirical material reality. Glissant, in my view, not unlike his critics, the creolites (Confiant, Chamoiseau), comes closest to uttering the Truth of the Americas and their creole-ness. Similarly, one might make the leap from Glissant's creole-ness to arguments about queerness as a relation of non-relation to Africa, the colonial legacy, and the post-colonial condition of imposition and disappointment and its sexualized orienting behaviors.

Why the queer ideas of Glissant? He writes as follows:

Creolization, one of the ways of forming a complex mix — and not merely a linguistic result — is only exemplified by its processes and certainly not by the contents on which these operate ... We are not prompted solely by the defining of our identities but by their relation to everything possible as well — the mutual mutations generated by this interplay of relations ...[24]

In his ideas rest the links to help us think about the melancholic morass of Caribbean homophobia and simultaneously its assumed heteropatriarchy along with "rights talk." The debates taking place in the region and its extensions concerning homophobia are only so banal in that feminist insights, many of them homopoetic (just recall Lorde's Zami or Crichlow's buller man, or Als' auntie man), still occupy an edge in politics and thought — in political thought and organizing. My surprise that feminism occupies the edge in the queer "rights talk" debate in the Anglo-Caribbean and its extensions tells me something about the work to be done and Dunsford's desire to see Lorde's work carried forward in Glave's anthology.

In the extensions much is possible including the production of what Glissant terms "the chaotic network of Relation and not in the hidden violence of filiations."[25] Are Caribbean cultures and their extensions more homophobic than others? The obvious answer is no. Yet, as one reads the 2004 Human Rights Watch report

"Hated to Death: Homophobia, Violence, and Jamaica's HIV/AIDS Epidemic," the question hovers for me like a hammer about to strike. In such a context, questions of liberation and rights seem clearly crucial. And, significantly, identities also appear to be at stake since the violence unleashed is specifically targeted at identities called into being through the very violence that seeks to make them non-existent. Glissant writes: "The ruins of the Plantation have affected American cultures all around"[26] — and such violence animates the complexities of identification on questions and practices of liberation. So, for example, every August 1, I hover between Toronto's Caribana celebrations in honor of Emancipation Day and Montreal's *Divers/Cité* celebrations in honor of contemporary queer subjecthood. I am caught between "the pleasures of exile" and the ethical demands of diaspora privileges to utter truth claims concerning Black and queer identities and possibilities, and their conjoined existence in my life; which is to hover in the gaps, spaces, and crevices of the Caribbean's multiple and contradictory inheritances of its queer formations, queer realities, materialities, identities, and sexual practices.

Against rights: A revision of sorts

The story of the last forty years of queer organizing in the West is one that has now been fundamentally reduced to a story of rights. What Miriam Smith calls "rights talk," the phrase I have been using, has dominated the ways in which queers think about themselves within the nation-state.[27] But "rights talk" has also become the model upon which the template for queer "liberation" across the globe now unfolds. The year 2009 marks the fortieth anniversary of Stonewall, the now mythic signifier of the modern gay and lesbian movement in North America, which has come to be characterized as the origin of the contemporary movement for queers globally. While the impact of North American and Western European queer organizing cannot be denied, its global impact as a template for liberation needs to be cautiously and suspiciously viewed, especially among its Western poor cousins in the Caribbean basin. Stonewall as an origin story works as a narrative in a very specific fashion. The narrative goes something like this: first there was queer repression; second there was gay rebellion and liberation; third there was rights talk; and now we/queers in the Western world are free and full citizens (with marriage in Canada, Spain, etcetera.)[28]

Such normative queer history posits gay liberation as infancy and rights talk as adulthood and maturity. In such a trajectory, people of color, Caribbean people, and people from the global south are, according to the Western historians, sociologists, political scientists, cultural critics, literary critics, and so on, still at the sexual liberation stage (if even there) — at the childhood stage. The undertones of some reviews of Glave's anthology hint as much. This developmental understanding of the place of people of the global south in the modern lesbian and gay movement is modeled on a notion that they/we are just now "coming out" and therefore still exist in some Neanderthal state of sexual repression and underdevelopment — a progress narrative if there ever was one. Thus, in book after book that chronicles the queer history of the movement over the last thirty years, people of the global south arrive at the literal end of the discussion as the last set of persons and bodies to come into their queer-ness. This enduring coloniality of queer life deliberately positions queers of the global south as needing a helping hand from the North Atlantic that is most times not about genuine struggle to build community but, as Spivak puts it in "Righting Wrongs," "that they must be propped up."[29]

I want to convey my ambivalence about rights talk as a mode of citizen-making for sexual minorities and non-heterosexuals. But I also want to point to a certain kind of insidious language of tolerance and niche-making that robs social movements of their potential to more deeply transform the nation-state and the disciplinary apparatus of citizenship. In liberal democratic societies, citizenship is the terrain over which governing is most aptly contested. Thus, any real and sustained changes to citizenship have an impact on all regardless of gender, sexuality, class, and so on. Queer rights to citizenship, then, must and should be a fundamental priority, but how those rights are attained is crucial for their sedimentation and cemented-ness to the nation-state. How these rights are attained has become crucial for what kind of human we might and can become beyond the present expansion of what Wynter calls the "ethnoclass" of Western bourgeois society.[30]

While Stonewall is credited as the origin story of

the modern gay and lesbian movement — and it is clear that Stonewall represents a significant and fundamental shift in queer self-assertiveness in North America — I want to offer a slight but different shift in reading the history of the movement. In my slight revision, I want to suggest that the advent of HIV/AIDS is the moment that captures the real energies made possible by the outpouring of the carnal pleasures that Stonewall unleashed. Stonewall was queer sexual liberation, alongside heterosexual liberation, but HIV/AIDS was citizen-making; the distinction is important. HIV/AIDS worked to produce a very particular and specific queer subjecthood. It was a subject who was sick and diseased in a fashion different from how homosexuality as illness had been previously conceived (even though in some people's view one illness led to the other) in the "eventful moment" of AIDS. Thus, it is in the realm of sickness and death that a very specific queer subjecthood comes into being. This queer subject also becomes a rights-seeking subject. It is my argument, then, that Stonewall was not the central route through which a modern queer citizenship took hold. Rather it was in the initial impetus/moment of AIDS in which a "proto-queer citizen" was forced to react and respond to the "stealing" of his carnal pleasures that rights talk and citizen-making became a queer project of self-hood and thus state citizenship. It is in that moment and distinction that my ambivalence lies in relation to rights talk concerning sexual minorities and non-heterosexuals.

Similarly, in the Caribbean region, rights talk is being

produced in the contexts of HIV/AIDS programs and services. Death and its after-effects are playing a significant role in the desire for "rights." Let me pose a few questions. What does it mean to claim rights in a moment of crisis? What does it mean to claim rights in the context of death? What does the claiming of rights under such conditions do to the exercise of those rights? What kinds of subjects are made when rights are claimed under such circumstances? While I cannot answer all those questions, I must say that we can glean a cautionary tale from what rights talk has produced for "post-rights" queer people in North America. These "post-rights" queer people measure their citizenship in the exact and minute terms of heterosexual citizenship. Any deviation from the heterosexual state norm is considered a lack in equal citizenship. Thus, the production of homonormativity does not just mirror heteronormativity, it also constitutes a knowable and therefore consumer population or niche that is and can be internally and externally policed and governed. This is something we must all think very carefully about, since I would argue that equality as a concept does not necessarily mean same treatment, same measures.

Tracy Robinson, much like Alexander, raises the question of rights as a question for Caribbean feminist thought and practice. In her discussion, rights citizenship comes under close scrutiny, and she contends as follows:

> The renewal of a meaningful discourse about citizenship in the Caribbean will show that,

notwithstanding the gender neutrality of many citizenship laws in the Caribbean and the language of equality implied in Caribbean constitutions, men remain the paradigm of citizen and, in significant measure, women are included as citizens through their relationship to men.[31]

Such feminist insights on citizenship have much to lend to conversations and debates on queer citizenship. It is my contention in the remainder of this essay that North American lesbian and gay citizenship has mirrored that of heterosexual citizenship but that even to achieve such it had to produce itself as a consuming and white male citizenship, at least in the popular imaginary. Robinson's discussion of how rights and citizenship both congeal and at the same time part ways is useful for debates concerning gay and lesbian citizenship as well. As she writes, "the liberal version of citizenship as a bundle of rights are misconceived if in the first instance we view rights as having some indubitable meaning, stabilized in law, that we can then quantify in degrees of personhood."[32] Nonetheless, Robinson "does not disavow rights discourse,"[33] and I would suggest that my argument that follows is not disavowal either but a caution about rights and identities or what she calls "personhood."

Rights talk, then, tends to reproduce the big "S" state with its various inequalities. By this I mean that rights talk provides space for elites within states to self-express; in the global liberal democratic south, such self-expression is definitely viable as well; but it might be argued that rights talk does not work for the poor; rights talk often works to produce and police sexuality on singular terms forcing sexual minorities into a one-size-fits-all model; rights talk will often produce space for those who are mobile in this newer version of globalization to enjoy their privileges across different spaces (as we see with the continuing controversies about queer cruises throughout the Caribbean); in short, rights talk comes with benefits, but those benefits in no way threaten the hegemony of state organization nor force the state to change its fundamental disciplinary apparatus of citizenship. Instead, rights talk most often asks that queer citizenship mirror heterosexual citizenship. Heteronormativity and homonormativity collude in policing sexually desiring bodies, practices, and communities in a tacit "sexual contract" with the state. A homopoetics of selfhood is not possible under those terms. The complexities of creole selves must be forcibly submerged, discredited, and even deemed deviant.

The Canadian queer sociologist Gary Kinsman provides a nuanced reading of how the nation-state can work for and against sexual minority political desires. Kinsman analyzes the various ways in which state policies and narratives create complex and shifting positions of exclusion and inclusion. Simultaneously, he is also clear that much queer organizing in the Canadian context reproduces the inclusion/exclusion model for a range of tolerated and not tolerated identities and sexual minority identities. Kinsman points out that a systematic study of state formation would point to the ways in which various forms of oppression are embedded in the making of the state. Drawing on queer legal theorist Carl Stychin, Kinsman writes about conceding to some state practices in a war of position: "According to his insightful investigations of the intersections of nation, sexual identity, and rights discourse ... state formation may be able to address social differences through its recognition of difference and tolerance of diversity."[34] However, Kinsman is intent on proving with caution how modern state formation is an anti-queer project even when it appears to include queers. He adds the following:

> This does not mean, however, that lesbians and gay men have not been able to exert agency and win gains within these state relations. Hegemony has never been total or secure. We have made important gains, but these gains have been limited.[35]

Kinsman's analysis is informed by a radical critique of the ways in which the market or late capitalism has had an impact on the formation of the nation-state and thus the sometimes partial toleration of once reviled identities. Dennis Altman's celebration of the "global gay" is often a tourist/consuming queer.[36] Such a queer keeps colonial capitalist relations in place. Kinsman's analysis suggests that toleration, rights talk, and the social and political gains that have been made are not sufficient. Thus, he concludes as follows:

In the end, we need to organize against the state form itself, which is based on constructing a series of relations that stand over and against people in our everyday lives, and that actively prevent us from gaining democratic control over the social circumstances of our lives.[37]

Kinsman's insights on Canadian nation-state formation as a practice of oppression that is often mirrored in lesbian and gay political organizing itself are important given where I write from and the ways in which such lesbian and gay organizing has often happened in the face of ignoring critiques from queers of color.

Conclusion: After rights, what?

Thus, if we return to the developmental model, we see that what is at stake is an assumption on the parts of both heteronormative and homonormative constituents that the extension of rights is the primary way in which queers might enter full citizenship. While many are familiar with the problem of rights and how rights work, the desire for them still remains a modern phenomenon. Rights must not only be granted but the granting of rights must be enforced. And even when rights are enforced, there is no guarantee that attitudes will change. Thus, what we get in the context of the juridical reordering of queer life is a wholesale acceptance of the status quo of social, political, and cultural organization of the society. But this should not surprise us, for queers are as desirous of the heteronormative dream as anyone else. Thus, in effect, homonormativity comes to mirror heteronormativity not primarily in its organization but in its desire to reproduce the privileges of the colonial/imperial nation-state in its various manoeuvres to retain its hegemony globally.

But the truth of the matter is that public reaction to queers, as an imagined constituency — that is a population — remains volatile, even hostile.[38] Toleration can very quickly turn into intolerance. Thus, toleration is dependent upon pleasing those who have extended it to you. But what is most important for me is that the global south remains conceptually outside the category of lesbian and gay as articulated in the North Atlantic. Thus, the insinuation that queers in the global south are still in the infancy of the movement is not as surprising as it might at first appear. Such a conceptual framework in the literature runs parallel with the popular representation of queers generally as white, middle class, and Western. And yet it is queers of the global south who continue to keep sexuality in flux, often offering some of the most provocative ways of reimagining what sexual minority practices might look like and what kinds of politics might be required to secure those practices: think of the much maligned down-low as one such case of keeping sexuality and its attendant identities in flux.

The question becomes: under what conditions might social movement happen? As I suggested earlier, the contemporary gay and lesbian rights movement in the North Atlantic owes a debt to the enormous tragedy of early

AIDS deaths. Those deaths were characterized by a public sphere backlash to the carnal pleasures of the late 1960s and 1970s sexual liberation movements. In the moment of backlash politics and the threat and misunderstanding of HIV/AIDS, queers were forced to secure methods through which they would not be forced back into "the closet." The range of instances, which can be catalogued as health care assurances, insurance policies and health benefits, estate law, and partner/civil agreements, all combined to make use of death and illness to reform state practices. All those reforms, however, mirrored those of heterosexual, state-sanctioned practices. These reforms did not launch any profound rethinking of the role of the state in sexual matters. Thus, queers emerged as a marketing niche for a range of capitalist and state practices. Rights through illness is a tricky business. It is no wonder, then, that most often queer rights in the North Atlantic are linked to consumption and the mythical pink dollar. The question remains: can or should this method of rights talk work as a template for the Anglo-Caribbean? Queers became tolerated as a market, not as sexual beings. As Wynter would put it, merely a new genre of the human,[39] which can only be dissatisfying in terms of how modernity and its motives have structured human life.

While a case can be made and has been made for the Caribbean as the engine of Western modernity — its plantations, the modes of freedom and unfreedom that characterized the region, the multicultural citizenry of the Haitian revolution, the post-Emancipation shifts in racial demographics and cultural forms, sharing, borrowing, and mixing on numerous levels (to name a few) — the Caribbean remains shut out of the West as a contributor to rethinking modern citizenship and the work citizenship does, both pleasing and disappointing at the same time. Let me suggest that as the Anglo-Caribbean queer movement hitches its future to the promise of rights that the liberal democratic nation-states of the region currently deny, the conceptual and actual flaws of modern nation-states become even more searingly apparent.

If, as I have suggested, HIV/AIDS is a central organizing dynamic of contemporary Western gay and lesbian rights talk and its institutions, the Caribbean case might both advance this claim and cause rights to be even more deeply problematic as a vehicle for liberation. As Kamala Kempadoo notes in her assessment of various studies on Caribbean sexual practices in the time of HIV/AIDS:

> It has, however, carefully raised the issue that homosexuality or gayness is not an uncommon feature of Caribbean societies — that Caribbean men engage in a variety of sexual activities with other men as well as women. These findings, taken together with widespread practices of informal polygyny and transactional sex, have led to analyses of complex sexual networks through which multiple men and women are seen to be sexually connected.[40]

Following up on Kempadoo's observation, one

might argue that sexual practices in the Caribbean are so far removed from the call to an identity that even mobilizing around HIV/AIDS as the means toward rights is a limited endeavor if founded on the North American model. In the Caribbean, the subtle refusals of heterosexual monogamy do not provide a model for a Caribbean homonormativity to mirror, thus creating a "queer" niche market and all of the other constitutive elements that make a community knowable and identifiable. This is counter to the North American and Western European model of sexual citizenship and the extension of rights as a group benefit by identifying oneself individually and collectively as a known quantity for citizenship. Thus, the Caribbean situation poses an ethical dilemma for the North American model. Second-order diasporas can best contribute to the ethics of the situation by being both cautious and sceptical about what rights and the experience of gay and lesbian rights have meant for their sojourns in North America and the European West.

Citizen practices and their state bestowal call for knowable identities — that is how the managerialism of citizenship works. However, sexual practices both multiple and varied, as we all know, do not require a manageable identity for their practice. Contemporary human rights are based on a claim to identity — a knowable identity. The ethics of the situation calls for rights without identity claims, a much more difficult set of politics to actualize. As Spivak writes: "Indeed, the name of 'man' in 'human' rights (or the name of 'woman' in 'women's rights are human rights') will continue to trouble me."[41] Sexual practices without attendant identities and a move that advances such a claim can pose new and important questions for the re-making of the late modern state. The Anglo-Caribbean queer movement has the potential to make such a contribution to our sexual politics in the twenty-first century.

Acknowledgements

I wish to thank Gayatri Gopinath and Andil Gosine for encouraging me to do this work on the region. Additionally, I would like to thank Gayatri and James A. Schultz for inviting me to the LA Queer Studies Conference organized by the UCLA Lesbian, Gay, Bisexual, and Transgender Studies Program on October 10-11, 2008, where I presented a version of this paper. The anonymous reviewers' comments were helpful in reworking this essay.

Originally published in *Caribbean Review of Gender Studies: A Journal of Caribbean Perspectives on Gender and Feminism*, Issue 3, 2009. http://sta.uwi.edu/crgs/currentissue.asp

Notes

1. Spivak, "Righting Wrongs," 551
2. Glave has consistently chronicled, collected, and sent out to the contributors any reviews of the book that he has come across. Additionally, the book recently won a Lambda Literary Award
3. "Re-membering our Caribbean connections: An Indigenous Maori Response to Thomas Glave's *Our Caribbean: A Gathering of Lesbian and Gay Writing from the Antilles*." http://www.apwn.net/index.php/news/more/review_of_our_caribbean_a_gathering_of_lesbian_and_gay_writing_from_the_ant/
4. See for example the opening paragraphs of M. Cornelius' review in *The Bloomsbury Review*, September/October, 2008, 19
5. *Words to Our Now*
6. This work does not seek to deny or occlude the multiracial and multicultural realities of the Anglo-Caribbean. Rather, since I identify as a Black Canadian of Caribbean background and my scholarship has largely centered on the dynamics of blackness in North America, I refer to Black people in this text as a formation of peoples that I know best. However, it might be useful to appreciate that in many North American spaces when the Caribbean is invoked, the blackness is also the first thing that is fundamentally imagined. However, it is important to note that many have called such imaginings into question (myself included)
7. Ahmed, *Queer Phenomenology*, 11

8. For developments of this line of thinking, see Neville Hoad's *African Intimacies* and Joseph Massad's *Desiring Arabs*

9. Mercer, "Decolonization and Disappointment," 116

10. Walcott, "Black Men in Frocks: Sexing Race in a Gay Ghetto (Toronto)"

11. Fanon, *Black Skin, White Masks*, 180

12. Als, *The Women*, 9

13. Ibid., 9

14. Ibid., 29

15. Wynter, "1492: A New World View"

16. Eribon, *Insult and the Making of the Gay Self*, 79

17. Crichlow, "History, (Re)Memory, Testimony, and Biomythography: Charting a Buller Man's Trinidadian Past," 186

18. Eribon, *Insult and the Making of the Gay Self*, xv

19. Glissant, *Caribbean Discourse*, 120

20. Ibid., italics in original, 120

21. "Rethinking 'Aesthetics': Notes Towards Deciphering Practice."

22. Alexander, *Pedagogies of Crossing*, 27

23. Glissant, *Poetics of Relation*, 16

24. Ibid. intertext in the book without a page number

25. Ibid., 144

26. Glissant, *Caribbean Discourses*, 72

27. Smith, *Lesbian and Gay Rights in Canada.*

28. The recent debacle with Proposition 8 in California and the initial reaction to the "Yes" side victory, in which the "No" side blamed Black and Latino/a voters, is another way in which it is assumed that Black

and other globally south people are in need of development when it comes to questions of queer sexuality. In many of the debates right after the election, one would have found it impossible to image Black and Latino/a peoples as queer subjects as well. It was eventually shown that blaming any particular racial group made no sense since proving it was not statistically possible

29. Spivak, "Righting Wrongs," 542
30. "Unsettling the Coloniality of Being/Power/ Truth/Freedom"
31. Robinson, "Beyond the Bill of Rights," 232
32. Ibid., 242
33. Ibid.
34. Kinsman, "Challenging Canadian and Queer Nationalism," 209-210
35. Ibid., 210
36. Altman, *Global Sex*
37. Kinsman, "Challenging Canadian and Queer Nationalism," 227
38. Rayside, *Queer Inclusions, Continental Divisions*
39. "Unsettling the Coloniality of Being/Power/ Truth/Freedom"
40. Kempadoo, *Sexing the Caribbean*, 170
41. Spivak, "Righting Wrongs," 564

References

Ahmed, Sara. *Queer Phenomenology: Orientations, Objects, Others*. Durham: Duke University Press, 2006.

Alexander, M. Jacqui. "Erotic Autonomy as a Politics of Decolonization: Feminism, Tourism, and the State in the Bahamas." In *Pedagogies of Crossing: Meditations on Feminism, Sexual Politics, Memory, and the Sacred.* Durham: Duke University Press, 2005.

Als, Hilton. *The Women.* New York: Farrar, Straus & Giroux, 1996.

Altman, Dennis. *Global Sex.* Chicago: University of Chicago Press, 2002.

Cornelius, Michael G.. *The Bloomsbury Review*, September/October (2008): 19.

Crichlow, Wesley. "History, (Re)Memory, Testimony, and Biomythography: Charting a Buller Man's Trinidadian Past." In *Interrogating Caribbean Masculinities: Theoretical and Empirical Analyses*, edited by Rhoda Reddock, 185-222. Jamaica: University of the West Indies Press, 2004

Dunsford, Cathie Koa. "Re-membering our Caribbean Connections: An Indigenous Maori Response to Thomas Glave's *Our Caribbean: A Gathering of Lesbian and Gay Writing from the Antilles.*" http://www.apwn.net/index.php/news/more/review_of_our_caribbean_a_gathering_of_lesbian_and_gay_writing_from_the_ant/

Eribon, Didier. *Insult and the Making of the Gay Self*, translated by Michael Lucey. Durham: Duke University Press, 2004.

Fanon, Frantz. *Black Skin, White Masks.* New York: Grove Press, 1967.

Glave, Thomas. *Words to Our Now: Imagination and Dissent.*

Minneapolis: University of Minnesota Press, 2005.

Glissant, Èdouard. *Caribbean Discourse: Selected Essays*, translated by Michael Dash. Charlottesville: University of Virginia Press, 1989.

———. *Poetics of Relation*, translated by Betsy Wing.. Ann Arbor: University of Michigan Press, 1997.

Hoad, Neville. *African Intimacies: Race, Homosexuality, and Globalization*. Minneapolis: University of Minnesota Press, 2007.

Human Rights Watch. *Hated to Death: Homophobia, Violence and Jamaica's HIV/AIDS Epidemic*. 2004

Kempadoo, Kamala. *Sexing the Caribbean: Gender, Race and Sexual Labor*. New York: Routledge, 2004.

Kinsman, Gary. "Challenging Canadian and Queer Nationalisms." In *In a Queer Country: Gay and Lesbian Studies in the Canadian Context*, edited by Terry Goldie Vancouver: Arsenal Pulp Press, 2001.

Massad, Joseph. *Desiring Arabs*. Chicago: University of Chicago Press, 2007.

Mercer, Kobena. "Decolonisation and Disappointment: Reading Fanon's Sexual Politics." In *The Fact of Blackness: Frantz Fanon and Visual Representation*, edited by Alan Read. Seattle: Bay Press, 1996.

Rayside, David. *Queer Inclusions, Continental Divisions: Public Recognition of Sexual Diversity in Canada and the United States*. Toronto: University of Toronto Press, 2008.

Robinson, Tracy. "Beyond the Bill of Rights: Sexing the Citizen." *Confronting Power, Theorizing Gender: Interdisciplinary Perspectives in the Caribbean*, edited by Eudine Barriteau. Jamaica: University of the West Indies

Press (2003): 231-261.

Smith, Miriam. *Lesbian and Gay Rights in Canada: Social Movements and Equality-Seeking, 1971-1995.* Toronto: University of Toronto Press, 1999.

Spivak, Gayatri. "Righting Wrongs." *Southern Atlantic Quarterly*, 103:2/3, spring/summer (2004): 523–581.

Walcott, Rinaldo. "Black Men in Frocks: Sexing Race in a Gay Ghetto (Toronto)". In *Claiming Space: Racialization in Canadian Cities*, edited by Cheryl Teelucksingh. Waterloo: Wilfrid Laurier University Press, 2006.

Wynter, Sylvia. "Rethinking 'Aesthetics': Notes Towards a Deciphering Practice." In *Ex-iles: Essays on Caribbean Cinema*, edited by Mbye Cham. Trenton, NJ: African World Press, 1992.

——. "1492: A New World View." *Race, Discourse, and the Origins of the Americas: A New world View*, edited by Vera Lawrence Hyatt and Rex Nettleford. Washington: Smithsonian Institute Press, 1995.

——. "Unsettling the Coloniality of Being/Power/Truth/Freedom: Towards the Human, After Man, Its Overrepresentation—An Argument." *CR: The New Centennial Review*, Vol. 3, No. 3, Fall (2003): 257-337.

Chapter 7

Diasporic Citizenship
Against the Rules of Blackness:
Hilton Als' *The Women* and
Jamaica Kincaid's *My Brother*
(Or How to Raise Black Queer Kids)

The title of this essay pays homage in part to Eve Kosofsky Sedgwick's 1991 essay "How to Bring Your Kids Up Gay." Sedgwick's essay is a reading of revisionary psychoanalysis and psychiatry in the post–DSM III excision of homosexuality as pathology. The third edition of the American Psychiatric Association's *Diagnostic and Statistical Manual*, published in 1980, replaced the identification of homosexuality alone as a disorder with one of "ego-dystonic sexual orientation," or one in which sexual orientation is in conflict with self-image. She argues that the attempt to normalize adult homosexual bodies is simultaneously an attempt to render gay bodies not present, and she suggests that this is done through an attempt to pathologize youthful sexualities. Sedgwick's critique of "the new psychiatry of gay acceptance" is cautioned by her readings of medical discourses on gender-disordered youths or youths who might be gay. The result of her against-the-rules reading and interpretation is the difficult knowledge that post–DSM III medical discourse finds so-called gender-disordered youths to be abnormal and in need of repair or fixing, even in the era of adult gay recognition.

Thus, Sedgwick's reading goes against the commonsensical rules of contemporary understanding, which now appear to assume that there is such a thing as a "normal" and "proper" gay and lesbian body and thus person. The implications of her interpretation are important for making sense of the discomfort with contemporary gay and lesbian bodies and persons that continues nonetheless.

For my purposes, such a reading by Sedgwick opens up both the presence and the absence of queer discourses and subjects within the context of Black diaspora discourses, Queer discourses in Black diaspora studies remain against the rules, out-of-order utterances that trouble the borders of the "normal" and "proper" Black body. That "normal" and "proper" Black body is an imagined heterosexual Black body. But the absent/present dyad that exists in Black diaspora studies does not and cannot entirely eliminate what we might tentatively call a Black queer diaspora. However, some of us have ventured to consider how such a Black queer diaspora comes into being. Or as Sedgwick puts it in a different but related context, "There is no unthreatened, unthreatening theoretical home for a concept of gay and lesbian origins."

In this essay I pursue the absented presence of a Black queer body through readings of Hilton Als' *The*

Women and Jamaica Kincaid's *My Brother*. These two non-fiction texts interestingly intersect with concerns around mothering, queer sexualities, and diaspora circuits and might be said to elliptically probe "Black gay origins." Importantly, these two texts might be read as against the rules of blackness because of the ways in which they attempt to "normalize" queer sexualities within blackness. By this I mean that these texts write against a heterosexual mythic blackness that, when confronted with the evidence of Black queers, crumbles miserably in the face of its sexual other. I read these texts as against the rules of blackness because, as Robert Reid-Pharr states, writing about Gary Fisher, "The Black gay man is then an object of attack not because he represents that which is horrid but because he represents one location at which the possibility of choosing one's identity (even within the most oppressive conditions) becomes palpable." The absented presence of the Black queer body, then, is so because such a body represents a counter to the desired respectability of the heterosexual Black body. Both *The Women* and *My Brother* are about much more than I read them for, but it is important to note that both texts were published at the height of the Afrocentric debates and both ignore such debates to offer us a different view of blackness. This essay brings all those conversations into collision.

Therefore, this essay attempts to trouble the discourse of Black mothering, both actual and symbolic, within diasporic discourse. It does so as heroic Black motherhood encounters youthful queer sexualities that exist within and against blackness. Black mothers are endowed with the responsibilities of raising Black hetero-sexual children. But how might we make sense of the context when they fail to produce the proper Black subject? Here I respond to the interconnected discourses of heroic Black motherhood postulated by Afrocentrism and the role of Mother Africa contained in such postulations. In particular, I see a link between Afrocentric discourses of motherhood and the veneration of Mother Africa. Significantly such venerations become problematic in the face of queer sexualities, especially for boys, who in such discourses must be considered as less than men. Therefore, I turn to queer theory to marshal an argument of living Black queerness "as if." Queer life is an essential element of blackness, constituted both by its insistence on realizing itself and by discourses that seek to render it not present, which in fact work to acknowledge its presence.

To demonstrate the "as if" of Black queer life, I turn to Hilton Als and Jamaica Kincaid, who retrospectively show how queer childhoods are an essential element of blackness. Recalling such childhoods from the place of adulthood complicates calls for thinking differently about Black motherhood and ultimately Mother Africa. Does Black motherhood fail when queer kids appear? Can normative notions of Black motherhood account for Black mothers' rearing of Black queer kids? Further, I suggest and show that some discourses of blackness make such a possibility a problem for Black mothering. Thus, discourses of Black mothering in normative narratives refuse the possibility of queer childhoods. This essay argues against such claims.

Sedgwick's essay challenges us to conceive of social, cultural, and medical discourses that would allow for the healthy rearing of gay youths. She wants an "erotically invested affirmation of many people's felt desire or need that there be gay people in the immediate world." At the least, such a challenge takes queerness outside of the pathologizing discourse of its medicalization in terms of so-called youth gender disorders, which Sedgwick suggests are mainly targeted at boys. Instead we are faced with other kinds of questions.

Both *My Brother* and *The Women* revisit youthful sexualities. I suggest that by refusing to justify Black homosexuality, these texts place the origins of Black homosexuality in some relief, thus making homosexuality an immediate given. In both texts, the category of the child is a category to be troubled, as the child becomes an adult who lives a life outside the boundaries or rules of normative blackness and preconceived standards of sexuality and sexual practice.

More generally, in the context of Black diasporic discourse, homosexuality and therefore queer identities continue to be contested terrain. Afrocentric thinkers such as Francis Cress Welsing and Molefi Asante have argued that homosexuality among Black people is a learned European behavior. Asante wrote:

> Homosexuality is a deviation from Afrocentric thought because it makes the person evaluate his own physical needs above the teachings of na-

tional consciousness. An outburst of homosexuality among black men, fed by the prison breeding system, threatens to distort the relationship between friends … we must demonstrate a real antagonism toward those gays who are as unconscious as other people.

And further:

The rise of homosexuality in the African-American male's psyche is real and complicated. An Afrocentric perspective recognizes its existence, but homosexuality cannot be condoned or accepted as good for the national development of a strong people …. We can no longer allow our lives to be controlled by European decadence…. All brothers who are homosexuals should know that they too can become committed to the collective will …. The homosexual shall find the redemptive power of Afrocentricity to be the magnet which pulls him back to his center.

Thinkers on the other side of the argument have sought to demonstrate that homosexuality is as African as many other cultural retentions and practices that characterize Black diasporic life. I am not interested in those valences of the argument from either side in terms of the past existence or not of homosexuality. I am interested instead in the metaphor of diaspora as family and kin and what that means when we must account for living with queers "as if." Such a claim places motherhood as central, since motherhood is essential to kinship discourses.

Homosexuality exists among Black diaspora people, and that is what I want to probe, not its origins but what might be a necessary ethical stance to bring to the rearing of black queer youths. I want to probe the ways in which two authors writing memoir or (auto)biography figure queer sexualities in their texts. I am interested in a diaspora ethics and discourse that can move beyond the theme of toleration of same-sex desire to a place where, to slightly rephrase Sedgwick, an erotically invested queer blackness might be possible. Als' *The Women* and Kincaid's *My Brother* open up the possibility of an erotically invested queer blackness in very different ways, and each author makes present, following Sedgwick, a "haunting abject" of Black sexuality.

Als articulates a notion of Black women, especially mothers, that he calls the "Negress." He states that "the Negress has come to mean many things." Among these things are selfless, welfare and social-assistance recipient, good neighbor, godly, depressed, bearing many children, sexless, lacking in mental capacities but emotional, and a host of other qualities that both contradict and supplement the construction of the Black woman as other, especially the Black mother. Als is most explicit in his desire to write against the rules of normative blackness not only in his discussion of Black female representation but also in debate with and against Black women.

Als not only launches a particular critique of American social constructions of Black women; he also launches a critique of some Black feminists' positions. In fact, Als problematically claims that Black feminists, especially novelists like Toni Morrison, need and in fact reproduce the Negress as a significant feature of what he terms their angry and sympathy-seeking literature, a practice that he finds, at the least, troubling. And yet Als offers us something quite complex in his trope of the Negress when he states: "I have expressed my Negressity by living, fully, the prescribed life of an auntie man — what Barbadians call a faggot." He continues:

[This] is a form of kinship, given that my being an auntie man is based on greed for romantic love with men temperamentally not unlike the men my mother knew — that and an unremitting public "niceness." I socialized myself as an auntie man long before I committed my first act as one. I also wore my mother's and sister's clothes when they were not home; those clothes deflected from the pressure I felt in being different from them. As a child, this difference was too much for me to take; I buried myself in their clothes, their secrets, their desires, to find myself through them.

Als recognizes his Negressity from childhood; and his mother and sisters found his Negressity troubling, to say the least. This is the point that Sedgwick sets out to make when she writes that "the wish for the dignified treatment of already-gay people" is threatened by the discourses and practices of revisionist psychoanalysis and psychiatry, which treats childhood queer expressions as pathological. Als' mother and sisters operated from the assumption of queer pathology. But as Als takes us back to his childhood in a poignant manner, he writes: "Being an auntie man enamored of Negresity is all I have ever known how to be. I do not know what my life *would* be, or if it would be at all, if I were any different" (emphasis in original). Such a sentiment is a strike against a normative and proper heterosexual blackness. Such a claim exists within and against blackness, since Als is always already gay and Black.

What Als gives us is a problem of how to ethically take up the relation of the queer child to its mother. A mother who is both hated and loved simultaneously. Melanie Klein's insights on child individuation can help us make sense of Als' emotions. His working through of his sexuality and his recognition of his Negressity, even when he remains ambivalent to it, are not unlike Klein's conception of reparation. Reparation can be understood in its simplest form as the relation of love, guilt, and hate that the child must hold toward its mother in order to eventually individuate. The work of reparation, then, is to redirect guilt for destruction and separation or hate from the central figure of the mother to the difficult task and work of loving her again. For the work of reparation to begin, we must acknowledge that something has been destroyed or would be destroyed. And in Klein's view, the work of separation is the work of the infant.

Reparation therefore becomes the means through which guilt is reduced and displaced, making the possibility to love at separation possible and even evident. It is in this manner that Als' *The Women* is an homage to women of various sorts: his mother, the first Negress in his life; Dorothy Dean, a very interesting pre-Stonewall "fag hag" who organized the social calendars of some of New York's most prominent and influential white gay men; and Owen Dodson, an important figure of the Harlem Renaissance. In addition to reading Als against himself, the work is an homage to the black feminists he feels compelled to engage and critique. We are then left with the question: is Negressity a form and expression of love?

Finally, Als' contradictory identification with the Negress and his taking on of an aspect of her identity — "romantic love with men temperamentally not unlike the men my mother knew" — might be understood as positing the argument that Als is suggesting a different take on queer normativity. In this version of queerness, Negressity is not a malady in need of or requiring treatment but a state of being that requires a space for a more active acknowledgment.

Als ups the ante on readers in his discussion of his cross-generational affair with his mentor Owen Dodson. He meets Dodson when he is thirteen and writes: "I was nineteen the last time we allowed this intimacy to happen between us. I was nineteen when I left him forever." The intimacy and mutual sharing of this cross-generational relationship raise many questions concerning how to bring kids up queer and Black.

Remembering his childhood from the place of

adulthood, Als addresses the crisis language of role modeling, denying that Dodson was a role model or father figure to him. And then Als offers us something more for thinking with. Warren Crichlow has pointed out that much role-modeling discourse is premised upon a pathologizing of blackness and Black people. It is accessing what the something more of Als is that I am attempting to arrive at. I suggest that the something more is a profound critique of Black diaspora normative claims of heterosexual kinship. However, I want to tentatively state that that something more might be merely how to make queer kids, to borrow from Doty's title, perfectly queer. Als writes: "One sister in particular (the one most like me) criticized our relationship beyond recognition. She said: 'He's turning my brother into a faggot.' I remember how I tried to avoid my sister's scorn by not speaking of Owen, and how often I saw him, how often the dust floated around our joined lips." Als' refusal to situate his sexual and other desires within any frames of normativity or respectability opens up for consideration ethical concerns. His refusal to make sense of himself as anything but a Negress is crucial for thinking about the ethical imperatives of his claims and insights. And whenever ethical concerns arise, rules are at stake.

In speaking of ethical concerns, I mean to signal a complex web of concerns that speak to the context in which Black queer sexualities might be conceived as belonging within the category of blackness. Michel de Certeau writes of ethics, "With ethics, social practice becomes the area in relation to which a theory of behaviors can be elaborated." I am convinced of de Certeau's formulation of ethics as "a theory of behaviors," because embedded in such a formulation is a theory of relationality and relation.

Social relationality requires an ethical dispensation, that is, a behavior that recognizes our responsible relations to one another. What that looks like is always in the process of being revealed. Both Als and Kincaid open up the concern of our responsible relation to one another on the terms both of sexuality and sexual practice and of kin and community. In this way, the ethical always pushes toward a something more that is awaiting revelation in the form of social behavior and conduct but can never fully utter its end point, for there is no end point in the realm of the ethical; there is only ongoing social relationality and responsibility.

Thus, the something more of Als' account that we must contend with is this: "It is only now that I attempt to let slip past the identity they have established for me, as their younger sister, and into a narrative that, even as I write, rejects my intellection, my control, because I betrayed its central character so long ago: Owen. Back then, I did not say to my mother and sisters: I am already a faggot." Such an account requires more than the nature/nurture debate can offer. Such an account takes us into the Foucaultian realm of care of the self and an ethics for living. Such an account requires us to think differently about childhood. I shall return to this later. But Als' account requires ethical thought. It requires that normativity in any guise be questioned or at least seriously grappled with. It requires that we take the child's utterance seriously, if only in retrospect.

Jamaica Kincaid's brother died the year *The Women* was published. Kincaid's *My Brother* comes to the issues or tensions discussed above from another place. In her impressionistic memoir of her brother who died of HIV/AIDS, the ubiquitous evil/loving mother haunts each scene. Anyone familiar with Kincaid's fiction or nonfiction knows that mothers, and her mother in particular, always represent a certain "problem-space" within her texts. There is no sentimentality for her mother or mothers. *My Brother* is no different in those terms, except that one might argue that the representation of the mother this time around creates a bit more space for seeing other sides of her. For example, Kincaid makes clear in the text that her mother felt that it was her duty to look after her dying son, to move him into her home from his shack in the back of her house, and to care for him every day when he was in the dilapidated hospital ward in Antigua. Yet Kincaid still critiques her mother for inhibiting her children's growth. This critique of her mother is evidently in conversation with Kincaid's anxieties about her own role as a mother to her children, whom she must leave in Vermont when she takes the HIV drug AZT to her brother in Antigua; and, she tells us, she sometimes prefers a book to children. Childhood is thus a general and troubling problem for Kincaid, alongside mothers.

Kincaid's brother died of HIV/AIDS in Antigua in 1996. After she made many trips to Antigua to deliver

AZT to him, his health improved for a while and then faltered again. As his health improved, so did his desire for sex and his desire to practice sex. In her book, Kincaid remembers that at the time of her brother's death, she could not write about him, because "I could not think about him in a purposeful way." Yet she gives us a memoir to help us think about his life and its broader implications in a purposeful way. It is the purposefulness of *My Brother* that I pursue in this essay.

Kincaid learned of her brother's sexuality, or rather the secret of her brother's sexuality, not in Antigua, where he lived his whole life, but while she was on a trip to Chicago promoting one of her new books after his death. On that trip, Kincaid encountered a woman who remembered her from an HIV/AIDS workshop in Antigua, and it was she who revealed evidence of her brother's sexuality to Kincaid. The revelatory passage in her book orients much of what I have to say here:

> And then she said that she had been a lesbian woman living in Antigua and how deeply sad it made her to see the scorn and derision heaped on the homosexual man; homosexual men had no place to go in Antigua, she said, no place to simply meet and be with each other and not be afraid; and so she had opened up her home and made it known that every Sunday men who loved other men could come to her house in the afternoon and enjoy each other's company. My brother, she said, was a frequent visitor to her

house, a safe place to be with each other; and my brother who had just died was often at her house, not as a spectator of homosexual life but as a participant in homosexual life.

Up until that point Kincaid had every reason, she tells us, to believe that her brother was heterosexual. Kincaid's claim lies somewhere between what Samuel Delany might call "the margin between the claims of truth and the claims of textuality." It is with sadness that she writes:

> He has died without ever understanding or knowing, or being able to let the world in which he lived know, who he was; that who he really — he was — he could not express fully: his fear of being laughed at, his fear of meeting with scorn of the people he knew best were overwhelming and he could not live with it all openly.

Kincaid knows all too well what revealing his nonheterosexuality to everyone would have meant for her brother in Antigua. At stake were a care of self and an ethics of living conditioned by a community's inability to do more than repress and punish the possibility of something other than opposite-sex attractions. Kincaid's brother continued to pursue opposite-sex attractions even when he was forced to acknowledge his HIV/AIDS status. His own deep refusal, on some level, of the complexities of his sexual practices was part of the "problem-space" of an ethics of living "as if." His own refusal of sexual and diseased categories also made the rules of sexuality and illness a difficult context for ethical consideration.

The question of mothering is played out in a context much larger than that of how we understand mothering. I therefore suggest that at stake are the question of kin and kinship and the larger question of family. In fact, I want to suggest that part of the problem of Black diaspora Afrocentric discourse is that the discourse of family is too bound up with it. Kincaid gives us an example from the first person in Antigua to publicly acknowledge his HIV status, a man named Freeston. Freeston made his seropositive status public in an effort to perform a public service. Kincaid recalls a visit with him:

> One day I was visiting with him and we were sitting on the gallery of his mother's house, a group of older school boys passed by and they called him an auntie-man and in other ways referred to his homosexuality, using vicious language; they were a chorus of intimidation, of scorn, of ignorance. Freeston was too ill to be upset, he was quite used to it ....
>
> His mother came from that generation of Antiguan women (older, around my mother's age or older) who did not know of homosexuality, or any kind of sexuality. To say that he was gay or homosexual was something he said about himself; to say that he was an auntie-man was something

people said about him. She understood him better when he was the person people said something about, not when he was the person who said something about himself.

Kincaid makes clear the link between family, community, and the "thing that dare not speak its name" — homosexuality. The above passage demonstrates the inability of the structures of family to work without the structure of community naming. Community thus takes on a kind of "mothering role," in this case the role of the evil mother, for this is not a mother that allows a healthy separation from her. She must brutalize before the separation occurs. This is not a heroic mother figure. The Kleinian bad-breast theory becomes applicable here. Community in this sense is unable to allow for a kind of erotically invested sexuality not marked as heterosexual; not even his biological mother can at that point identify with Freeston. This inability to recognize Freeston or to recognize him except as an insult places him against the rules of blackness: his existence is outside assumed normative blackness.

Kincaid continues, nonetheless interestingly complexifying mothering: "But whatever people said about him, whatever he said about himself, it did not matter to his mother; she took care of him, he lived with her in a house with a beautiful garden full of zinnias and cosmos and some impatiens and all sorts of shrubs and with glossy and variegated leaves. She was so different from my brother's mother." Although Freeston's mother is the antithesis of Kincaid's, she is still bound by community standards as she tries to make sense of her son. It is this larger question of community as mother that I finally turn to.

I want to make at least three points by way of three different theorists. In 1983, Cheryl Clarke wrote an essay titled "The Failure to Transform: Homophobia in the Black Community," in which she analyzed the limitations and failures of any potential Black revolution within the US context as lacking in its ability to deal with and acknowledge the complexities and diversities of Black sexualities, especially lesbian and gay sexualities.

Some thirteen years later, in his essay titled "Decolonisation and Disappointment: Reading Fanon's Sexual Politics," Kobena Mercer, following Clarke, argued that sexual politics remained "the Achilles heel of black liberation." What these two essays share is the theme, and emotion, of disappointment, but disappointment as the ground upon which a more hopeful politics might be desired. These essays also share a concern about liberation so that life can be lived "as if." Embedded in both arguments is a tacit acknowledgment of family or at least kin, as well as a larger and more important discourse of community. Both essays also offer a critique of some forms of Black nationalism as it morphs into the Afrocentrism of the late 1980s to mid-1990s, in which I am particularly interested here.

In turning to the third theorist, Melanie Klein, I want to take up mothering metaphorically and politically, as yet another aspect of the Achilles heel of Black diaspora desires and antagonisms. A major part of the problem with discourses of blackness in the Black diaspora can only be worked out by working through the difficult and unrelenting relation to Mother Africa. In this regard, I want to suggest that until Black diasporans make reparation with Mother Africa, the local contexts of mothering, not to mention myriad other relations, will remain deeply fraught. Making reparation with Mother Africa requires a healthy separation so that something of the New World Black might be revealed.

Stuart Hall has identified at least two different approaches to Black diasporan identity that inform this condition. The possibility of such reparation is only evident when the latter of the two versions of cultural identity and diaspora that he identifies comes into play. Hall argues that the first version centers Africa and the enforced conditions of diaspora. In this version, "Africa is the name of the missing term, the aporia, which lies at the center of our cultural identity and gives it a meaning which, until recently, it lacked." In this version, the discourse of "loss of identity" via the forced migration into slavery in the Americas opens up a discourse of healing that concerns itself with peeling away layers of oppression to arrive at a core identity as is often articulated in Afrocentric thought (for example, by people like Welsing and Asante). On the other hand, a second version of identity acknowledges the intervention of history. This intervention of history can be, and is, the basis upon which a healthy separation might be achieved. Thus, Hall cautions us that diaspora is also about departure and that departure does not merely signal origins, that is, Africa and having left it. Instead, departure might signal "axes or vectors … the vectors of similarity and continuity; and the vectors of difference and rupture." These vectors signal the more nuanced and complex facets of diaspora identities. Hall further states: "Diaspora identities are those which are constantly producing and reproducing themselves anew, through transformation and difference."

I suggest that it is the second version of diaspora identity that allows for the making of reparation with Mother Africa. Furthermore, any return to Mother Africa for New World Black peoples must simultaneously be a break with Africa as well. For many, this is to flaunt the rules of origin, to be against blackness, but I am interested in the attempt to come to terms with oneself as emblematic of what Paul Gilroy terms the counterculture of modernity. Such an understanding of blackness displaces conversations of origins in a certain and stable homeland in favor of thinking about origins as process and importantly embedded in the violent and traumatic making of the Americas. Here I am not suggesting that Africa is outside the modern. In fact, if we follow Valentin Mudimbe, any invocation of the term "Africa" suggests an invention of the modern. This effort to make reparation, then, is an attempt by New World Blacks to work through their relation to the Americas. Working through their relation to the Americas cannot, then, be conditioned by a search for an authentic African sexuality but rather might concern itself with the "new" and recombined sexualities of the Black diaspora — the second version of identity. Such an approach places Africa as one position within a narrative of the past and opens up other positions for identification as well. For example, one of those other positions might be the tragedy of HIV/AIDS as a kind of glue to the formation of a Black queer diaspora.

Constituting queer as a diaspora is problematic. As Alan Sinfield has argued, queers do not find one another because of a trauma that united them into a particular historical narrative that they might use as the basis for the making of community. Sinfield argues, and correctly so, that despite the numerous atrocities that some queers are exposed to on the occasion of coming out, these are not the kinds of trauma that make a diaspora. I think Sinfield's argument works better for Euro-American queers than it does for Black diaspora queers. I have argued elsewhere that HIV/AIDS is a pandemic for which there is no outside, which means that we are all positioned in relation to it, whether or not we have sex. Thus, a Black queer diaspora might exist as a kind of typology of desire as opposed to an empirical reality.

HIV/AIDS connects New World Blacks to Africa in myriad ways, from the stereotypically racist representations of AIDS and its origins to planetary activist politics around its spread and treatment. I want to propose, therefore, that the fluidity of HIV/AIDS allows for a New World Black disposition whereby identifications useful beyond the desire and insistence of homeland and/or origins discourse can produce some kind of common feeling or connectivity. In this sense, New World

Black persons can model an identity or activate new identifications accessed in the Americas cross-culturally as a place where, as Sylvia Wynter argues, "new forms of human life" come to be; this is so even if it happens through the tragedy of the HIV/AIDS pandemic. But new forms of human life also suggest new relations of mothering and motherhood, in short, a new set of rules.

Both Hilton Als' *The Women* and Jamaica Kincaid's *My Brother* inaugurate New World Black reparation, because both texts refuse the posture of representing Black queer sexuality as a special effect in need of repair, especially in its youthful eruptions. Each text takes seriously the old adage "rules are made to be broken" and breaks the rules of normativity, respectability, and assumed blackness. But even more importantly, both texts refuse to be surprised by Black queerness. This is in fact the fundamental place that Sedgwick might see as how to begin to live within a culture for which no explanation for queerness is necessary. This is against the rules of the human as presently constituted. To offer no explanation for queerness, especially its childhood utterances, would be to live against the rules, for the rules require an explanation; to offer none is to invite questions, concerns, even violence.

I am ultimately suggesting that such a culture, *a Black queer culture of "as if,"* is only possible when reparation is made both in terms of Mother Africa and in terms of actual Black mothers both generally and locally. Both texts, I believe, attempt to make reparation and thus to enable separation and love for mothers locally.

Diasporically, the general situation that requires a healthy break with Mother Africa is achieved not through the old-time Black conservative tropes of hatred, shame, and denial of and for Africa, nor by Afrocentric glorification and veneration, but rather by affixing the place that Africa works for and is called upon to play in all forms of Black diaspora desires. Until that historical trauma is worked through or continually worked upon, any other discourses concerning mothering will remain troubling, indeed faulty, for diaspora Black peoples; and young and other Black queers will remain beyond and against the rules of the category Black.

Originally published in *Sex and The Citizen: Interrogating the Caribbean*. Faith Smith (ed.). University of Virginia Press: Charlottesville and London, 2011, 75-86.

References

Als, Hilton. *The Women*. New York: Farrar, Strauss & Giroux, 1996.

Asante, M. K. *Afrocentricity*. Trenton, NJ: Africa World Press, 1988.

Clarke, Cheryl. "The Failure to Transform: Homophobia in the Black Community." In *Dangerous Liaisons: Black, Gays, and the Struggle for Equality*, edited by E. Brandt. New York: New Press, 1999.

de Certeau, Michel. *The Writing of History*, translated by T. Conley. New York: Columbia University Press, 1988.

Doty, Alexander. *Making Things Perfectly Queer: Interpreting Mass Culture*. Minneapolis: University of Minnesota Press.

Gilroy, Paul. *The Black Atlantic: Modernity and Double Consciousness*. Cambridge: Cambridge University, 1993.

Hall, Stuart. "Cultural Identity and Diaspora." In *Diaspora and Visual Culture: Representing Africans and Jews*, edited by Nicholas Mirzoeff, 21-32. New York: Routledge, 2000.

Kincaid, Jamaica. *My Brother*. New York: Farrar, Straus & Giroux, 1997.

Klein, Melanie. *Love, Guilt, Reparation and Other Works, 1921-1945*. London: Virago, 1988.

Mercer, Kobena. "Decolonisation and Disappointment: Reading Fanon's Sexual Politics." In *The Fact of Blackness: Frantz Fanon and Visual Representation*, edited by Alan Read, 115-131. London: Institute of Contemporary Arts; Seattle: Bay Press, 1996.

Mudimbe, Valentine. *The Invention of Africa: Gnosis, Philosophy, and the Order of Knowledge.* Bloomington: Indiana University Press, 1988.

Reid-Pharr, Robert F. *Black Gay Man.* New York: New York University Press, 2001.

———. "Tearing the Goat's Flesh: Homosexuality, Abjection and the Production of a Late Twentieth-Century Black Masculinity." *Studies in the Novel 28*, no. 3 (1996): 372-94.

Scott, David. *Refashioning Futures: Criticism after Post-coloniality.* Princeton, NJ: Princeton University Press, 1999.

Sedgwick, Eve Kosofsky. *Epistemology of the Closet.* Berkley and Los Angeles: University of California Press, 1990.

———. " How to Bring Your Kids Up Gay." *Social Text 9*, no. 4 (1991): 18-27.

Sinfield, Alan. "Diaspora and Hybridity: Queer Identities and the Ethnicity Model." In *Diaspora and Visual Culture: Representing Africans and Jews,* edited by Nicholas Mirzoeff, 95-114. New York: Routledge, 2000.

Walcott, Rinaldo. "Queer Texts and Performativity: Zora, Rap and Community." In *Queer Theory in Education,* edited by W. Pinar, 133-45. Mahwah, NJ: Lawrence Erlbaum Associates, 1998.

Wynter, Silvia. "1492: A New World View." In *Race, Discourse, and the Origin of the Americas: A New World View,* edited by V. Lawrence and R. Nettleford, 5-57. Washington, DC: Smithsonian Institution Press, 1995

Chapter 8

Black Queer Studies, Freedom, and Other Human Possibilities

Introduction: Thinking Black Death

As the terrible legacy of the Middle Passage continues to shape the conditions of Black diaspora subjects, the question of death should be central to the analysis of Black diaspora cultures. Coming into being in the midst of the death-dealing of transatlantic slavery, New World Black being is founded in and through death, as HIV/AIDS and, more largely, Black Queer Studies still prove today. A thought experiment based on the work of diaspora artists, this essay intends to address this claim and its corollary: Black people die differently. It is my contention that the historical relations that produced Black peoples are the same relations that produce their deaths.[1] Such claims mean that thinking blackness requires we pay attention to how and why Black people die, when and where we die. Why Black people die differently from others. When we consider health care, illness, crime, prisons, poverty, or any of the social markers that make life livable, Black peoples' experiences of those social markers are radically different and thus lead to a different kind of death. For Black peoples, death cannot be minimized and, in contemporary culture, it remains an intimate element of Black life and living always in view. Radically different from the universal outcome of all human beings' lives, *Black death* is constantly framing Black peoples' everyday livability — even more acutely for Black poor and Black queer people.

In any major North American city, for instance, the numerous "missing" Black women (presumed murdered), the many "missing" and murdered Transwomen, and the violent verbal and physical conditions of Black life often leading to the deaths of gay men, lesbian women, and Trans people remain a significant component of how Black life is lived in the constant intimacy of violence on the road to death.[2] Death is not ahead of blackness as a future shared with other humans; death is our life, lived in the present. Should you think this too stark a claim about Black life, recall the way in which state violence as practiced by police forces can at any time take a Black person's life with impunity. Thus, it seems clear to me that those of us engaged in critical scholarship might turn our critical lens to death and why Black death is a different sort of dying. In this essay, I am attempting such a shift — from looking at some works through the lens of identity to reading them through their engagement with death and their lessons for different kinds of human possibilities.

Marlon Riggs' Lesson on Dying

In *Black is … Black Ain't* (1994), Marlon Riggs' body is decaying right before our eyes. As viewers, we get to witness his death in action, only because friends and colleagues complete his last will and testament to the idea that "black is black ain't." Marlon Riggs decays before us, dying in the frame of the camera as he united life and death — his life, our coming deaths, in a filmic text that requires viewers to engage the ethics and desires of seeing and witnessing. Riggs' *Black is ... Black Ain't,* then is obviously a film about life and its intimate relationship to death. In Riggs' final statement on Black ontology/ies, he positions both desire and ethics as central to late modern articulations of Black being and the politics of the gaze that frames, shapes, and fashions our encounters with Black subjects. *Black is ... Black Ain't* moves fluidly from singular to plural in its insistence on singularity as the force through which the difficulties of community might become possible and how we might gaze on his HIV/AIDS disease and dying body. His disintegration beckons to our own coming deaths and simultaneously requires us to command an ethics of and for living life.

Such a shift from identity to an ethics where death is central informs my reading of a Black queer image-archive in the same way as the late Barbara Christian worked through Morrison scholarship and challenged it thoroughly. In her essay "Fixing Methodologies: *Beloved*," she worried about and explored the tremendous amount of scholarship that greeted Toni Morrison's *Beloved.* Christian was curious about what such an enormity of scholarship might teach us about the text across the various methodologies that were being used to discern Morrison's profound mediation on the question of blackness in the US. Christian was concerned about the ways in which she felt a rather complex text was being appropriated in ways that did not seriously tackle its complexity. In her critique, then, Christian takes the bold stand to suggest that the text (she refuses to call *Beloved* a novel) is one concerned with "ancestor worship"[3] and to propose that *Beloved* was more than a novel, it was indeed a prayer. Drawing on West African cosmology and specifically on the work of religious philosopher John Mbiti, Christian points to the ways in which such a cosmology remained partially intact for the descendants of those who crossed the Middle Passage. Most importantly, she argues that death was not an end in itself, but that the dead lived on in other worlds in which forms of communication remained possible given the brutalities of the crossing and the kinds of deaths they experienced. If modern blackness is thus founded in death, it is not so as a coming to terms with what it means to be human or even with a desire for freedom from human wordliness, but it rather comes into being through an inability to lay its dead to rest in the throes of unfreedom.

Christian writes: "In not being able to remember, name, and feed those who passed on in the Middle Passage, those who survived *had* to abandon their living dead to the worst possible fate that could befall a West African: complete annihilation."[4] Christian then suggests through her reading of the epigraph of *Beloved* ("To the sixty million and more") that the entire text is a "fixing ceremony."[5] I would add to Christian's insight that the opening sentence of the text, "Not a story to pass on," also signals a deep structure of Black ontological struggles concerning embodiment. Such a ceremony as

Beloved must take death or dying as central to collective well-being and healing and also as practices intimately bound up with living, if anything resembling a livable life is approachable.

In Michele Wallace's obituary of Marlon Riggs, she honestly revealed that she often asked herself why his flame was turned up so high. Wallace in retrospect acknowledged that she did not immediately realize the urgency in Riggs' work. In a film like *Non, Je Ne Regrette Rien (No Regret)*, in which five black HIV-positive gay men discuss their fight against homophobia and AIDS-phobia, Riggs dealt with death in a fashion that required viewers to think about how Black dying is different. The film features lips, hands, teeth, and even fruit-themed poetry as a way to encapsulate the humanity of Black gay men, men dying, decaying from HIV/AIDS. The work of the film offers a different kind of Black embodiment in which history, struggle, and defiance mark the sites of Black queer possibility in the face of racist-homophobia from white queer communities and Black homophobic communities. The film is indeed a prayer on the terms that Christian would recognize. Made at the height of the pandemic, *No Regret* (38 min, 1993) is a film about death as a frame for Black human-ness and freedom. The film asks viewers to engage with how our livability is conditioned by the deaths of others. Riggs' lesson for living, then, requires us to engage an ethics of mutual political responsibilities in which queer sexualities are not other to a normative hetero-blackness or a white queer subcategory.

The Thought of Black Death

Death is a marker of Black diasporic life — not a conclusion but its very origin or foundation. It is indeed a poetics of diasporic subjecthood across a range of conditions, expressions, and desires, and thus foundational to our histories. The crossing of the Atlantic inaugurates our intimate relation to death in a fashion that I believe is different from many human others. Our ancestors' deaths became our lives, their deaths our troubles and desires to set them free, and thus our freedom is tied to them as well. Such "histories" or intimacies condition Black diaspora lives, and our and their relationship to dying and death becomes the condition for life and living. Significantly, Black ontologies fashion our desires for witnessing and indeed for engaging an ethics of care conditioned through the move toward death as central to Black being. Black concerns with being human are always premised upon the intimacy of death, and therefore an ethical relation is produced in the context of refusing a life that is a living-death. Indeed, one might argue that Black subjecthood, most often described as Black resistance, is conditioned against the always looming threat of being made the walking-dead. More significantly, I am suggesting that Black (gay) artists have inherited from their ancestors, or put another way, simply from their past, a poetics of care of the self that frames how some contemporary Black artists engage the "dark and lovely" subject of the Black image.[6]

This essay is about what I call the homopoetics of

Black death. This idea of homopoetics comes to me through engagements with the late Édouard Glissant. He wrote: "I define as a free or natural poetics any collective yearning for expression that is not opposed to itself either at the level of what it wishes to express or at the level of the language that it puts into practice."[7] Glissant begins to formulate a notion of poetics that I find useful to begin thinking a Black diasporic homopoetics within the Americas. I am interested in the ways in which theories and studies of queerness, discourses of sexuality — especially gay, lesbian, bisexual and Trans — create ephemeral conversations but also affect the deep structures of Black being to produce communities of sharing and political identifications across a range of local, national, and international boundaries of desire and sex, all brought together through death and dying. For me, homopoetics is the practice and analysis of how Black queers relate (or not) with other queers all the while producing modes of being that are both in concert with and against hegemonic gay and lesbian identities, homonormative inclusion, and Black homophobia. It is in part my argument that Black queer image-making contributes significantly to homopoetic relations and identifications across the Black diaspora.

I am thus similarly interested in the bodies that circulate across and within the Atlantic and Caribbean zones of the Americas and the places and spaces those bodies occupy — imaginary and otherwise — as central to a homopoetics of relation. This interest in thinking "the Black homosexual of the Americas," or what I will call "the homopoetics of relation," following Glissant, is particularly urgent and sensitive as HIV/AIDS continues to be a significant defining feature of the Afro-Americas, alongside an alleged "Black homophobia" exemplified by claims of a "violent Caribbean homophobia." Jamaica, for instance, has been deemed one of the most homophobic places in the Black diaspora, and its dancehall has been dubbed "murder music."[8]

Glissant is interested in movement. Thus, my insistence in this essay as well as other work is to refuse national boundaries and roam the Black diaspora as a method of reading post–Middle Passage Black life. Such movement allows for tracking the ways in which the conditions of Black death seem to repeat across space, time, and location. In turning to Glissant, the idea is not to queer him but to work with his already rather queer theories and insistences to make links, if also ephemeral, of the relation or non-relation of thought, as a method or an exercise of making the political appear. In such fashion, Riggs' insistence on requiring us to think death through witnessing his own is analogous to Glissant's poetics of relation in that they both ask us, indeed require us, to think relation and singularity as the condition of plurality. They also mean that we should consider thought as the act of non-relation producing relation and proximity, as formations and foundations for an ethics of living together. It is indeed such moves, such conditions, that constitute what I call "homopoetics." In part, I am suggesting, again influenced by Christian, that what is at stake are different conceptions of time, memory, and the past. Importantly, time, memory, and the past for the Black subject are the very conditions lived intimately in the present, thus Black diaspora peoples are always in the future, the future is never just ahead of us.

Glissant claims two kinds of poetics: natural and forced. He proceeds to more fully define natural poetics as:

Even if the destiny of a community should be a miserable one, or its existence threatened, these poetics are the direct result of activity within the social body. The most daring or the most artificial experiences, the most radical questioning of self-expression, extend, reform, clash with a given poetics. This is because there is no incompatibility here between desire and expression. The most violent challenge to an established order can emerge from a natural poetics, when there is con-tinuity between the challenged order and the dis-order it negates.[9]

Glissant offers in his articulation of a natural or free poetics a method for "reading" and debating that might be useful for thinking blackness, queerness, and claims of a deadly homophobia within and across Black diasporic communities in the Americas. It is a method of movement, of relation, and of thought. The move-ment is not merely one of bodies but ideas as well. The relation is not merely one of identity, it is politics too. The thought is not merely one of ideas and speech acts, it is a queer insistence or, as he puts it, it is a "that that." A "that that" requires living with the intimacies of violence as also formative of Black embodiment and Black being — it is just that way.[10]

The archipelago of the Caribbean is not merely a geographic space but rather an entity with a global reality, an extension in time and space, as well as into other places. It is indeed a queer geopolitical-imaginary-space that resists all sorts of normativities even when contradictorily reaching for the "normal." For those of us who have any relation to the region (and that is all of us in the post-colonial modern world) Sylvia Wynter has called "the archipelago of poverty," commitments can be complex and contradictory. Given the ways in which non-heterosexuality is often understood as outside the region in multiple ways, dilemmas abound when it comes to political expression and demands, cultural desires, and identifications or relationships between place, nation, and space — especially the extensions — that is, other Black diasporic spaces. Thus, Riggs has Haitian-American artist Assotto Saint literally perform no regrets in the film of the same name. Saint's refusal to rethink life in the face of an impeding death in the conclusion of the film as the credits roll is instructive. He performs David Frechette's poem "Non, Je Ne Regrette Rien" ("I Have No Regrets") and improvises on the poem, in which he defiantly refuses to regret one thing about the life he has lived as his body too decays from HIV/AIDS at the height of the pandemic. Saint tells us in searing tone, "I did it all ... back of trucks, bathhouses ... and I have no regret."

What I am pointing to is that these films, *No Regrets* and *Black is … Black Ain't*, act as a last will and testament, a homopoetics of relation in which the ethics of looking and living produces acts for living an ethical life in the aftermath of viewing these films. Such an ethical life would require modes of living that desire the conditions of freedom as central to achieving a satisfactory death. Importantly, these films offer those still living the opportunity to put their dead to rest in ways that they too might experience life differently in the aftermath. As Christian recommends, these films attempt the feat of "a coming to terms with" as a way to resolve and to take seriously "stories not to be passed on" given the historical troubles of the Black body.

The Science of Black Death

The Black body is always a body in trouble, and the queer works of the Kenyan-American artist Wangechi Mutu has thematized such troubles as complicated colonial and post-colonial monstrous protrusions of various sorts but especially pinpointing sexuality and sexual organs as central to the problem. The science used to mark the African/Black body as non-human is a "science of spectacle," as Katherine McKittrick reminds us, that lends itself to being resignified in narratives and images that refuse the subordinating intentions of scientific practices. Mutu's *Forensic Forms,* for example, mines the repeating history of the monstrous African/Black body, but with a crucial difference, one that allows us to make sense of our collective troubles with those bodies — for example,

Olympic champion Caster Semenya's body — as existing in a much longer story embedded in the "scientific spectacle" of modernity's encounter with Black bodies.[11]

As you might recall, Semenya, the South African distance runner, was accused of not being a "woman" because of her speed and her physical appearance. The controversy that ensued led to science being used to both "return" Semenya to how she always understood herself and, at the same time, suggest that she might not be entirely within the category of "biological woman." In Semenya's case, hormones become protrusions, not buttocks, labia, or penis to recall the founding stereotypes of Black sexuality.

Mutu's art is made of collage or "pieced together" from other images and found objects to form faces and bodies unimaginable, distorted, disturbing, and yet brutally real. The science of forensics is generally concerned with death and/or a "digging deeper" practice, but it can also be understood as concerned with history and as an art of piecing together. The work of the forensic scientist is to make sense of and to help to explain how the dead body came to be dead, and the fashion in which it died. Thus he/she must work backwards — that is, work out a history of what produced the dead body in the first instance — and at the same time explain the scientific techniques that made the narrative of death possible. Both method and practice, forensics is thus also a hypothesis that is conceptual. It is a representation — a different representation which informs our project of a homopoetics of relation and of Black queer deaths.

To think filmic and photographic representations as acts of thought that produce relation and as new modes of communication with community, with life, and with a demand for a new ethics of living is what shapes homopoetics where death is also an essential element of embodiment and subjectivity. These films ask viewers to come to terms with and to commit to practices for which the death-dealing horrors of modernity might be put to rest. Thus, the ethical demands of these works do more than represent identity, disrupt community, and unsettle heteronormativity. Instead, these films call for an encounter in which the urgency of the present confronts and resignifies a past so that the present is experienced differently. For example, when Riggs runs naked through the woods, he reconnects with nature but also with a narrative of an African past that is to be refused given the shameful nakedness of a backward and primitive Africa. Instead, Riggs exhorts us to own our bodies so that freedom might be felt and enacted differently. The naked body is reclaimed and exalted by Riggs in singularity as an attempt to rearticulate the symbolic collective need for new forms of Black embodiment.

Shooting Death

In many Black diaspora circles, to think about Black death and photography, the obvious choice might be to turn to James Van Der Zee, the photographer of the early twentieth century whose exquisite work on Black death is documented in *The Harlem Book of the Dead*, incidentally published by Toni Morrison when she was still an editor at Random House. However, I turn to Black queer photographers Rotimi Fani-Kayode (Alex Hirst) and Lyle Ashton Harris, whose work has been over-whelmingly read as concerned with questions of identity. I am in no way suggesting that previous work is off base; rather, I am concerned to see how we might think Black life and its death by reading these works through a different lens, so to speak. Photography as a practice and an art has a long historical relation to death and mythologies of stealing souls and other forms of bodily invasion. We shoot with the camera. For Black photographers, the practice of the machine and the production of the image is an existential struggle fraught with all the problems of the flat surfaces of representation and their desires to restate Black imagining. It is my conceit that such struggles are grounded in the *jouissance* (the pleasurable pain) of Black death. This particular insistence on pleasure and pain as co-constitutive is influenced by Susan Sontag's insistence that images of suffering have become central to our contemporary human life. I read Sontag against the grain to suggest the artists I am working with urge us to witness their suffering as a means towards our potential freedom.

The photographic evidence, extensive as it is, that exists of Black men's lynched bodies is a horrific documentary resource that tells as much about the spectators as it tells about those who have been brutally victimized. Writing on the photography and lynching, David Marriott observes that for the white male spectator, what "taking the picture can do and reveal about" the self is "a figure in a public event, a means to fashion the self through the image of a dead black man and the identification with fellow whites which can follow."

"At the same time, it is as if he wants to make an archive of what he sees, to preserve an event for the benefit of those who could not be there (friends, family, a son or daughter, perhaps)."[12] Black people, and particularly Black queer people, have worked with these desiring lenses to recapture and re-frame the photograph as a practice of the poetics of relations, a homopoetics of relation in gay hands, and an ethics of living life. These practices move beyond witnessing, these practices are constitutive, as I would suggest about the photographer, filmmakers, and other artists I mention above, of Black death and life.

As noted by Carole Boyce Davies in discussing Sylvia Wynter's work, the creative-theoretical is central to how we might make sense of these works. It is a way of making what Barbara Christian, in the essay "Race for Theory," had signaled as Black women's conceptual labor in their "creative works." Boyce Davies goes a bit further to demonstrate how "creative" works theorize and how "theory" is creative but also how both forms bleed into each other for Black diasporic artists/thinkers. The creative-theoretical demands we think both forms simultaneously, and it demonstrates that abstraction, difficulty, and intellectual reorientation do not only reside in the genre of theory.

It is my argument that Black queer artists are central to this paradigm. I return now to the two photographers

— Lyle Ashton Harris and Rotimi Fani-Kayode — to further push the importance of the creative-theoretical. I aim to further articulate the idea that an ethics of care and living is beyond witnessing. Indeed, these artists use their work to offer new and different modes of embodiment, which demonstrate how Black queer studies is founded in death — a post–Middle Passage ontology where the pandemic of HIV/AIDS shape, Black queer desiring subjectivities.

In *Black Visual Culture: Modernity and Postmodernity,* Gen Doy offers a symptomatic reading of the Fani-Kayode/Hirst collaboration, *The Golden Phallus.* While Doy is alert to the ways in which the image produces a relationship to HIV/AIDS and thus death and dying, he spends much of his time making the case for reading African mythology in the images and the means through which contemporary African art survives in an art market of exoticism. Doy's analysis is one method to think about the image, and a very legitimate one, so my difference here is not meant as a criticism. Rather, I want to further explore the strategy employed by *The Golden Phallus* for making us conjure up death and dying through placing the condom on a Black penis. In the age of HIV/AIDS, the Black dick has emerged as an instrument as dangerous as the gun. In the midst of the HIV/AIDS pandemic, a major Black photographer produces a work that visualizes, or at the least asks us to, as Essex Hemphill once put it, "think as we fuck."[13] Shifting to reading the image as one concerned with life and death, rather than other readings, opens up a different set of concerns in which

Fani-Kayode's art fashions the intimacy of death and life for Black diasporic peoples as a reparation with how we/they put "our dead behind us."[14]

Similarly, in the photograph *Bronze Head* (1980s), the Black buttocks (ass), presumably that of the artist, is being penetrated by an Ifa bronze head. In the context of HIV/AIDS and the various forms of "traditional" violence that might frame Black queer livability, taking it up or in the ass might signal a certain type of death. And while HIV/AIDS has in many ways become a Black disease globally, a "secret epidemic" among African-Americans especially, the questions of sex, death, and taking it up the ass remain central to Black livability. But again, as I have written elsewhere, HIV/AIDS is also for "new world" Black people a contemporary link or trace back to Africa, given that across historical time and space these multiple Black communities share intimately the devastating impact of the pandemic as a perverse way of making reparation and kinship with a past too horrible to pass on.[15] The virus globally decimates blackness wherever it might be found.

Lyle Ashton Harris' photographs *Constructs #10*; *Miss America Triptych*; and *America, Miss Girl, 1987-1988*, among other works, produce at first a sensation of a singular concern with identity, as noted by most critics. Yet, in keeping with my desire to move Black queer studies beyond identity to a fuller appreciation of Black (queer) freedom, I will read those images otherwise. Harris' donning of white face, while immediately a kind of Fanonian reference, reminds us that how we make sense of Black identities might indeed constitute life and death acts. But when a Black face is masked in white while a Black dick/cock is evident, other concerns become apparent: the need to make reparation and to think how death is constantly animating Black life. Indeed, Harris has invoked in at least one interview that identity exists as a "sacrifice." In such statements, I hear echoes of Christian's fixing ceremony discussed above. I (re)read these images and later work, then, not as fundamentally concerned with identity, but rather with death and reparation.

Significantly, then, these works work at the level of "ghosting," they mark a "time out of joint" to follow Jacques Derrida's lead and appropriate Hamlet. These works seek to transform the very thing they interpret,[16] and our interpretation of these works must be an ethical inclination to approach such a desire — to transform Black life as death approaches. The ghosting, spectral, conjuring qualities of these works enact a hauntological imperative that places the question of Black death front and center in our present time.

Conclusion

These works create an ephemeral imaginary and relation. Who is being imagined? What kinds of histories are being invoked? What constitutes Black queerness? Is Black queerness the body, culture, race, ethnicity, disease, all of the above, or only one of the above? These images offer a counter response and a counter-representation to the limited vocabularies and literacies being constructed and evoked in our contemporary conversations. This image economy refuses easy consumption from a range of positions and yet, the images articulate a demand for a different and better type of conversation. All these images speak at least twice, if not more, never settling — for they cannot — for a singular or a monolithic visual embrace that would never be sufficient. But all these images echo relation — a homopoetics of relation and an ethics of the singular care of the self-producing plurality and community.

It is, then, my argument that these works attempt a reinvention of the human on Fanonian terms — a desire for a new embodiment. Given the ways in which death, and, in this case, brutal deaths, shape and form Black diasporic life, these works ask us to grapple with the specificity of the anti-Black elements of modernity. Mutu's first solo exhibition, *This You Call Civilization?*, opened in Toronto the same month that Haiti's ongoing expulsion from modern globality was further exaggerated by the earthquake, reminding any of us who care to know and notice that the effects of that catastrophe have many of their roots in the brutal deaths and life of the most "African" of Caribbean spaces produced in the dreadfulness of transatlantic slavery. Haiti is one moment of the late modern's hauntology in which the spectacular evidence of Black death reminds us of the work that must be done in terms of a re-enchantment with and for the human — a new humanism beckons.

Finally, what I have tried to accomplish here for Black queer studies sits somewhere between the continuum of Lee Edelman's no future and José Muñoz's utopia.[17] While my own position is closer to utopia, I must state that in its demands about dying, Black queer livability is a command to move towards a future utopian possibility. As Marlon Riggs put it in "Unleash the Queen": "Gaze upon me. Gaze upon this deviant, defiant, diseased Other. T-cell count less than 150. The collapse of kidney function imminent from interior ravaging by multiplying microbes. Disease consumes me."[18] Riggs' homopoetics of decay and death continues to shape contemporary Black life, and most importantly across sexualities. His homopoetics is importantly a different embodiment, one that speaks its pain as potential freedom. In that moment, Riggs highlights how our lives can make no sense outside of his coming death, the collective deaths of Riggs, Joe Beam, Hemphill, and especially Audre Lorde. The foundations of a Black queer studies – demand to think desire and politics in the present as a way of making reparation with "our dead behind us." Such reparation allows for a life that can be lived with a freedom not yet felt, but one genuinely yearned for. Freedom as a way toward new ways of being human in the present, ways of being human in which Black life preceded Black death and is continually fashioned by death even before its birth — our embodiment takes place in the context of reckoning with life-death-world experience.

Originally published in A. Crémieux, X. Lemoine, and J. Rocchi (ed.). *Understanding Blackness Through Performance:*

Contemporary Arts and the Representation of Identity. New York: Palgrave Macmillan, 2013, 143-157.

Notes:

1. See the work of Clyde Woods, the Black geographer, in particular "Life After Death" (2002), and Joäo Costa Vargas, *Never Meant to Survive* (2008)
2. See the *Mailonline*, January 18, 2012 for a dramatic photo-collage of some of the many faces. But also see the Black and Missing Foundation for further information on this rarely discussed and commented on phenomena
3. Christian, "Fixing Methodologies," 6
4. Ibid., 13, emphasis in original
5. Ibid., 14
6. See Kobena Mercer, "Dark and Lovely Too: Black Gay Image Making" in *Welcome to the Jungle*, London & New York, Routledge, 1994
7. Glissant, *Caribbean Discourse*, 120
8. See *Hated to Death: Homophobia, Violence, and Jamaica's HIV/AIDS Epidemic*, Human Rights Watch, November, 16, 2004; "The Most Homophobic Place on Earth? Time, Wednesday, April 12, 2006, as examples of the way in which Jamaica also stands in for the entire Anglo-Caribbean in these conversations
9. Glissant, *Caribbean Discourse*, italics in original, 120
10. Glissant, *Poetics of Relation*, 159-167
11. *This You Call Civilization?* is the book produced from the exhibition
12. Marriott, *On Black Men*, 9

13. *Ceremonies*, "Now We Think," 155
14. See Audre Lorde, *Our Dead Behind Us*
15. Walcott, "Against the Rules of Blackness: Hilton Als's *The Women* and Jamaica Kincaid's *My Brother* (or How to Raise Black Queer Kids)"
16. Derrida, *Specters of Marx*, 51
17. Lee Edelman, *No Future: Queer Theory and the Death Drive*, Durham and London, Duke University Press, 2004
18. Riggs, "Unleash the Queen," 105

References

Christian, Barbara. "Fixing Methodologies: *Beloved.*" *Cultural Critique*, No. 24 (Spring 1993): 5-15.

———. "The Race for Theory." *Cultural Critique,* No. 6 (Spring 1987): 51-63.

Davies, Carole Boyce. "Preface: The Caribbean Creative/Theoretical." *The Caribbean Woman Writer as Scholar: Creating, Imagining, Theorizing,* edited by Keshia N. Abraham. Florida : Coconut Creek, 2009.

Derrida, Jacques. *Specters of Marx: The State of the Debt, the Work of Mourning, and the New International,* translated by Peggy Kamuf. London: Routledge, 1994.

Doy, Gen. *Black Visual Culture: Modernity and Postmodernity.* London: I.B. Tauris Publishers, 2000.

Glissant, Édouard. *Caribbean Discourse: Selected Essays,* translated by J. Michael Dash. Charlottesville: University of Virginia Press, 1989.

———. *Poetics of Relation,* translated by Betsy Wing. Ann Arbor: University of Michigan Press, 1997.

Hemphill, Essex. *Ceremonies: Poetry and Prose*. New York: Plume, 1992.

Marriot, David. *On Black Men*. New York: Columbia University Press, 2000.

McKittrick, Katherine. "Science Quarrels Sculpture: The Politics of Reading Sarah Baartman." In *Mosiac: A Journal for the Interdisciplinary Study of Literature*. (2010)

Moos, David. (Ed.) *Wangechi Mutu: This You Call Civilization?* Toronto: Art Gallery of Ontario (2010)

Riggs, Marlon. (1992). *No Regret (Non, Je Ne Regrette Rien)*. Frameline. 38 mins.

——. (1994). *Black is … Black Ain't*. California Newsreel. 87 mins.

Vargas, Joao Helion Costa. *Never Meant to Survive: Genocide and Utopia in Black Diaspora Communities*. New York: Roman and Littlefield, 2008.

Walcott, Rinaldo. "Homopoetics: Queer Space and the Black Queer Diaspora." In *Black Geographies and the Politics of Place*, edited by Katherine McKittrick and Clyde Woods. Toronto and Cambridge: Between the Lines and South End Press, 2007.

——. "Against the Rules of Blackness: Hilton Als's *The Women* and Jamaica Kincaid's *My Brother* (or How to Raise Black Queer Kids)." *Sex and the Citizen: Interrogating the Caribbean*, edited by Faith Smith. Charlottesville: University of Virginia Press, 2011.

Wallace, Michele. *Dark Designs and Visual Culture*. Durham: Duke University Press, 2004.

Woods, Clyde. " Life After Death." In *The Professional Geographer*, 54:1, (2002): 62-66.

Wynter, Sylvia. "Rethinking 'Aesthetics': Notes Towards a Deciphering Practice." In *Ex-Iles: Essays on Caribbean Cinema*, edited by Mbye Cham. Trenton, NJ: Africa World Press, 1990.

Chapter 9

Blackness, Masculinity, and the Work of Queer

Introduction: Why Black Masculinity?

What does it mean to be a Black man in late Western modernity? What does it mean to be a Black man in Canada in the contemporary moment? What are the markers of Black masculinity? Under what terms, figures, metaphors, tropes, ways of naming, specifying, and demarcating might we come to know Black men or know something about their masculinity and/or masculinities? A range of questions, concerns, confusions, ambivalences, and other kinds of conundrums sit in the conceptual background of this essay. The first and most significant is that there can be no legitimate claim made on behalf of a singular Black Canadian masculinity. Any claim of a Black Canadian masculinity could only assert a claim of Black masculinities, taking the plural substantively seriously across a range of ethnicities, classes, sexualities, regions, religions, and so on; and even then one could not be exhaustive about the dense diversities of Black masculinities present and operative in contemporary Canada.

This essay, then, is fraught with the complications of speaking Black masculinities as any kind of known quantity, at the same time as it takes seriously the insistence that Black masculinities exist and that thinking maleness, thinking masculinities, especially what has come to be called "hegemonic masculinities,"[1] is not possible without taking seriously the singularity of something we have also come to call "Black masculinity" as a significant singularity and crucial element of a "Black history" in the West and masculinities more generally. Since Black masculinity has as its adjective "Black," it immediately signals its constructedness and therefore its history and histories. The additive "Black" already begins to tell a story about masculinity. Despite claims to the contrary, hegemonic masculinity remains an unmarked masculinity whose history and histories must be read onto it, a history that it must be placed within, so that its unmarkedness does not continue to perpetuate the unremarkable nature of whiteness, or otherwise Euro-American patriarchal coloniality and its authority to name the world on its own terms as the only legitimate way to name all of human life.[2]

Therefore, the main thrust of this essay is to think through what contemporary Black masculinities and their study might add to the literature of and in masculinity studies. I aim to grapple with Black queer masculinities as central to all masculinities in a number of ways. The first way is by focusing on Black queer men. The second way is by demonstrating what and how Black queer Muslim masculinities can teach us about the ways in which masculinity, racism, and Islamophobia can conjoin to produce or make Black men "racialized others." Ultimately, I hope to demonstrate through those two moves that "Black masculinities" is a category that complicates studies of masculinities in a fashion that makes more recent categories like "racialized masculinity" somewhat nonsensical, as such categories continue to place non-white men in only oppositional and subordinate positions to both hegemonic white masculinities and the larger culture of coloniality, in which men of color make lives in a context that calls continually into question the conditions of their existence. This essay thus works out of the ruins of colonial histories and neo-colonial times to attempt to articulate the problematic contours of Black masculinities and by extension other non-white masculinities as authorizing subjectivities within and against narratives of knowing, which call into question larger paradigms of Euro-modernity's desire to name, categorize, and thus know and control.

The very language of "racialized masculinities" replicates a certain kind of colonial violence that refuses to differentiate between non-white peoples when it fits its interests. And, significantly, it places white hegemonic masculinities in a superior relationship to non-white masculinities, effectively articulating whiteness as outside the troubling category of race. In my view then, racialized masculinities do not bring non-white masculinities into view; rather, such a designation obscures the ongoing colonial conceptions of masculinities in general, privileging Euro-American hegemonic masculinities as the most legitimate modes of "Being" across class, sexuality, region, religion, and ethnicity to name a few modes of "Being."

Finally, this essay seeks to open up the ways in which we think social justice might be possible. To do so, the essay takes as its primary example Black queer Muslim subjectivities to articulate a notion of critical diversity as a mode of thought that might add something to the ways in which we conceptualize what the work of thinking social justice might require of us. This essay does not provide answers but instead offers probes as a way toward a different and, dare I suggest, a better conversation.

From Here to There and Back Again

Stephen Ducat in *The Wimp Factor: Gender Gaps, Holy Wars, and the Politics of Anxious Masculinity* argues along with many others that public articulations of virulent homophobia are still acceptable within public discourse in North America, especially in the USA. Such claims by Ducat and others are a cautious reminder that despite the tremendous reshaping of the post-Stonewall public sphere, a largely urban reshaping, the expression of hatred of queers in the public sphere is still widely accepted across many parts of North America. It was reported that on the occasions of both the invasion of Afghanistan and of Iraq, US soldiers wrote "faggot" on many of the bombs used in the initial bombardments. The evidence of such language in the initial opening of the war demonstrates that Afghans and Iraqis had to be reduced to the category of non-human, and one way to do so was to use the language of "faggot" to dehumanize them. The brutality of war does not just begin and end with bombs, but language or more broadly the deployment of ideas and ways of thinking plays a fundamental role in the production of the enemy and the practices of making others subordinate, less than human, and therefore worthy of death.

It might still be argued that many in North America still believe that homosexual sex is the ultimate derogatory human behavior, and the homosexual remains the most despicable human category for most globally still. Thus, to be reduced to the category of faggot is to occupy a place of non-human possibility for many. On this terrain, as well as many others, Christian fundamentalism and Islamic fundamentalism, among a number of other religious fundamentalisms, share much in common. It is abundantly clear that practices of dehumanization rely upon putting into place language and images that make the violence of dehumanization acceptable, palatable, and thus a necessary part of rendering one's enemy the other.

In our particular context of war — war waged on Afghanistan and Iraq, the constitution of the enemy/ other as "fags" points to, but not solely I would argue, anxiety at home as the public sphere increasingly becomes a site for the incorporation of a liberal articulation of gay and lesbian identity. One significant source of this would be the photos that emerged from Abu Ghraib. I am interested in the photos that came out of the brutal and dehumanizing torture in Abu Ghraib because those photos tell a longer and deeper history of the US racial imaginary. I am particularly interested in the photos that make use of what I will call, following Didier Eribon, "the homosexual insult." This interest is an attempt to make sense of the ways in which those photos coming out of Iraq spoke to an anxiety in contemporary North American culture concerning the "new" place of the homosexual in public life. I would suggest that the use of the homosexual insult as a form of terror, and an act of violence and thus intended trauma in Iraq, is as much about the place of the homosexual in contemporary North American culture, as it simultaneously represents a collapse of the liberal discourse of inclusion, which is fraying at its edges as queers articulate, demand, and expect more and more freedoms. It might well be argued, or at the least suggested, that the method of torture, in this case homosexual insult, is as much about US soldiers, mis-education about Islam and the Arab world as it is about a certain kind of inability and immobility to redirect a train that has already left the station in North America — in this case, the train is the articulation and increasing enshrinement of rights for homosexuals in public institutions and discourses in North Atlantic countries, what Anne McClintock might call "paranoid empire."[3]

But at home queers of color often fall out of those institutions or just don't show up. This is especially the case in the US Armed Forces, where large numbers of queer African-American and Latino/as serve and until recently worked under the "don't ask, don't tell" Bill Clinton policy. Thus, while contemporary North America boasts of LGBT rights and institutions as a central aspect of how its democracies work, at home, "mainstream" institutions often fail to provide adequate representation in its broadest sense for queers of color. Such inadequacies have significant consequences for how discourses of rights travel from North America to elsewhere and how queers of color in North America make sense of, participate in, and fashion queer subjectivities. In essence, in many instances, the lives of queers of color speak to the limits of rights claims in deeply profound ways.

In the institution I know best, the university, the above is particularly true. Over the last few years, I have had the opportunity to teach, to learn from, and to learn with an incredible and impressive group of Black queer and Black Trans students. These students live and work at the interstices of communities, studies, and politics, and in each case they are often not imagined as belonging, and in most cases they are rendered unbelievable. They, we, occupy the larger problem that all Black people are faced with, which is that of being both unimaginable in the academy and simultaneously unbelievable. While the academy is a place that fosters the imagination in a wide variety of ways, especially in scholarship, the academy is also a place that lacks imagination when Black people show up in it. Black people seem to produce the limit of the academy's imagination whether it is scholarship, policy, or just simple courtesies.

One of the many things that Black queer and Black Trans people learn very quickly in the academy is that none of the post-1960s offices (human rights, LGBT, disability, etc.) can contain them, can address their issues and concerns, and can adequately account for their presence as students, faculty, and staff. These offices, policies, and even studies, working tightly within the boundaries of, for example, LGBT identity, imagine their normative subject as always a queer Euro-North American subject. Such subjects are the beneficiaries of post-Stonewall rights cultures and institutions. A Stonewall story that has been recast as a Euro-North American "casting out" of Black, Latino/a, and other queers and Trans people of color from the triumph story of North American democratic redemption written as LGBT history. The Black queer subject cannot be imagined to exist, nor can such a subject seek services, be written into scholarship, and be intelligible to and in policy. The Black queer and Black Trans subject is indeed an unimaginable person-hood, unbelieved as even existing in actuality by some.

To make the claim from the subjecthood of black-ness that the academy lacks imagination when it comes to Black subjects, especially Black queer and Black Trans subjects, is not to cast aspersions on only the conservative side of the academy. Indeed, many on the "progressive" side of the academy find it difficult to imagine Black subjecthood too. Many a scholar working on the difficult questions that the post-9/11 security culture has thrown up for us has consistently and some might even say per-manently cast the Muslim body as a "brown body," mak-ing immediately absent and invisible, even unimaginable a Black and/or African Muslim body. I have elliptically written about this particular problem elsewhere in the essay "Reconstructing Black Manhood; or The Drag of Black Masculinity." However, I revisit some of those ideas here to throw the net a bit wider in an attempt to demonstrate the depth of the problem that the Black queer subject, the Black Trans subject, and all Black people encounter in the North Atlantic academy. As the photographer Abdi Osman has powerfully shown, the limits of our imaginations have significant implications for our politics of liberation, as I will demonstrate below.

Let us take as our example the Black or African Muslim. How might we think about Muslim positionality in Euro-North America? To help do the work of thinking critically about the ways in which Muslim subjectivity is both always already present and simultaneously elided in North America, we must confront what Wahneema Lubiano in the foreword to Ronald Judy's *(Dis)Forming the American Canon: African-Arabic Slave Narratives and the Vernacular* calls the "failure of categories." Both Judy's study and Lubiano's "muscular" engagement with the study's limits and possibilities point to the contested nature of how blackness and Muslim-ness come to be in the colonial Americas. Judy's study makes use of "linguistic indeterminacy"[4] as the premise of his investigation into how a Kantian, modernist "Reason" could not make sense of an enslaved Muslim presence, especially its representivity in Arabic and in the practice of Islam, which had to be vigilantly denied and invalidated for Christian doctrine to endorse slavery. The question of language as mentioned earlier repeats its history here. Thus, all enslaved Africans had to be reduced to the non-religious or Africans' practices of monotheism (in this case Islam) had to be ignored and denied since those practices troubled certain European reasons for African enslavement.

Reading the Muslim presence, then, as much more than a mid-twentieth century one in North America presents a different kind of intervention. It is an intervention that blackens and thus complicates a number of histories, trajectories, and politics. In this regard, the Muslim presence has a far deeper and more extensive and complicated archive than is currently being accessed by both the right and progressives alike in North America. This longer history and its elision haunt our contemporary conversations. Framed in this way, representivity is of utmost importance since the long history of Muslim presence in the Americas is in the first instance a Nigger, Negro, or Black one; and following Judy, it is a representivity that is both "linguistically foreign"[5] and heterographic. And it is crucially important to note it is a Black presence that speaks to the deeply profound ways in which the African body was not just stolen and made into a commodity but also it was fundamentally denied the status of body in the first instance.[6] This story of denying the African a body repeats in the Caster Semenya story, most recently when she was denied subjecthood through the limited imaginaries of race and gender only to be "rescued" by politics and science.

The question of the body takes its most potent form in contemporary politics concerning the Muslim body. The Muslim body, recently, resignified as a "brown body" in the context of post-9/11 discourses from a range of positions has made recalling the longer history of a "Nigger Muslim" presence in the Americas crucial. The failure of the category "brown body" to produce a thick representivity and performativity of Muslim-ness lends a certain indecipherability to Muslim-ness that might be productive for various kinds of interventions. Lubiano quarrels with Judy's otherwise brilliant study for its inattentiveness to gender and in particular the gendered nature of Kantian Reason.

I want to mobilize both Judy's and Lubiano's insights to position the queer images of the photographer Abdi Osman, which mediate against the continued invocation of a "brown-bodied" Muslim as a failure to produce an adequate response to what Toni Morrison calls the "the economy of stereotype." The photographs below point to the limits of the imagination and offer a profound critique of contemporary conversations about Muslim representivity and performativity. Much like the film *A Jihad for Love* (2007), the photographs reorient and re-open narratives elided and possible political claims and concerns glossed over. These "critical fictions" require us to imagine a different kind of past, present, and future. And since the photographs inscribe an iterative "queerness," they call up the multiple ways in which the scholarship my students are creating attempts to produce a conversation in the Euro-North America academy that might make them believable on some plane of thought. They, we, seek to regain our bodies from failed imaginations and practices.

Photos, Sex, History

Didier Eribon in *Insult and the Making of the Gay Self* argues that insults are instrumental to queer self-constitution both from the inside and the outside. Eribon persuasively demonstrates how insults work to both make a self that is recognizable by others and simultaneously a self that is identified by others, meaning to single one out as different from a norm. Thus, for Eribon, insult is not just the fun play of camp among gay men (in particular), but it is also a method of marking out difference and establishing a heterosexual norm. Many heterosexual men are forced to reinforce and perform heterosexism in fear of being, or as they are assaulted, regulated, and policed by the homosexual insult. Thus, the homosexual insult is a moral and violent regulating mechanism used on the one hand to secure heteronormativity, or at least its performance, and simultaneously to make queer selves evident and visible — it is brutally double-edged.

Eribon writes: "One of the consequences of insult is to shape the relation one has to others and to the world and thereby to shape the personality, the subjectivity, the very being of the individual in question."[7] Insult in this formulation is no small practice. As Eribon states, "insult is a performative utterance"[8] and "insult is a verdict,"[9] which suggests that insult does something and it works for something. Insult in relation to queer selves works to bring them into being and in many ways to maintain the being of presence. Insult among queers is as central to an imagined gay world as sexual practice is. Whether one is gay or not, it is quite common for one to experience being gay through the mechanism of insult. Thus, Eribon writes, "gay identity is always forced to remember its origins in insult as soon as it makes an effort to forget them."[10] Insult calls the queer into being (for example, "Look, a fag"), and just when the queer might have achieved a certain sense of self, for which sexual identity might not be paramount, insult can return one to one's origins (for example, "Gay men are spreading AIDS again"). These kinds of utterances keep queers within a circle of repetition and difference that depends upon forms of communication that subvert as those forms retain a sense of self, safety, and other necessary life resources.

Thus, Eribon suggests that queers learn to speak twice. By this he means to signal the mechanisms through which queers must often rework speech acts to blunt the violent impact of language. I will shortly suggest that Osman's photographs speak twice in a similar fashion to a range of failed categories. Since insult is meant to produce shame, gay men have also used insult as a way to produce a response to shame. Thus, insult within gay circles is an acknowledgement of the ways in which language and forms of communication work to dominate but also how language is a site of contestation and struggle. Language in the latter use works to take back assault and to produce forms of community and identification that render one intelligible to self and others in a constant negotiation of making multiple forms of human life possible.

Abu Ghraib stands as a monument to reducing human life in the Muslim and Arab world to a singular subordinated position. From colonial (i.e., Algeria) to contemporary imperial wars (i.e. Vietnam) of domination, we have a history of atrocities being enacted in situations where entire populations must be rendered suspect and thus the ultimate enemy when the dominating force is refused collective entry into the psychic life of a people alongside its forced entry into the people's material and everyday psychic lives. But this colonial logic has its origins in European colonial history, aboriginal genocide and near genocide, and transatlantic slavery, as Sylvia Wynter and others have taught us in their studies of coloniality.

Some of the earliest photographs of violence and sexual insult come out of the trauma of US segregation, and they constitute the earliest history of photographic technology as both archive of memory and something more. The photographs of lynching provide us a reference point for Abu Ghraib. The photographs of Abu Ghraib are the imagistic recall and the extension of the archive of photographs of lynching in many respects. Abu Ghraib is an extension abroad of practices from home, and such an extension must be read for how home figures in practices abroad. Thus, why homosexual insult? Why hooding? Why sexual organ display? Each of those questions points to the history of lynching in some form or the other as a significant aspect of the USA's racial unconscious. Similarly, the taking of photographs of one's victims has an intimate relation to lynching. Thus, the history of photography is deeply intertwined with the practice of lynching.

The photographic evidence (extensive as it is) that exists of Black men's lynched bodies is a body of horrific documentary resources that tells as much about the spectators as it tells about those who have been brutally victimized. David Marriott, writing on the photograph and lynching, observes that for the white male spectator, what "taking the picture can do and reveal about" the self is "a figure in a public event, a means to fashion the self through the image of a dead black man and the identification with fellow whites which can follow."[11] "At the same time, it is as if he wants to make an archive of what he sees, to preserve an event for the benefit of those who could not be there (friends, family, a son or daughter, perhaps). Wish you were here. A grotesque family album."[12] Marriott's analysis pinpoints the moment of the Abu Ghraib photographs. The overlapping colonial, segregated, and contemporary histories intertwine to produce a narrative which takes root in the non-human production of the Black.

To understand the historical reduction of the Black body to non-human status through the practice of lynching is only to grapple with one of the most debasing highlights of the colonial project. Native American genocide and its various attempts must also be systematically accounted for in this conversation. Abu Ghraib makes the history and the present touch each other and thus cohabit through the techniques of practices of non-human production exemplified by colonial conquest. Abu Ghraib might be read as one instance of the old in the new. But also stemming from colonial genocide, Native reservation entrapment, Black curtailment and lynching, and the prison industrial complex represent an almost seamless move from colonial Americas to US national borders to Abu Ghraib and back again.

Juxtapose those images of Abu Ghraib, too brutal to repeat their brutality by showing them here, with the archive of orientalist images that we are all very familiar with from movies, newspapers, and magazines and a range of other media sources and literary avenues, and the "ethnic notions" of racialization in the Americas become more availably present in our analysis. In this regard, artists working at the limits and impossibility of representivity, indeterminacy, and hybridity might provide some resources for a wider palette of literacies in a post-9/11 world. I turn to one such artist now.

Abdi Osman, whose work in the images below and other photographs not shown here, seeks to respond to the African/Black Muslim absence and invisibility by both asserting a presence and also complicating the presence through queerness, thus immediately disarming the stereotype of a violent Muslim masculinity that is practiced on "non-believers" and/or Muslim women. Again, the photographs also engage the question of unbelievability: of a queer Muslim, a Black/African queer Muslim, the place of queer Muslims in North America, their iconography, and so on.

A queer African Muslim himself, the photographer uses the lens to tell a story that complicates the images, forcing viewers to seek out histories either not readily known or easy to grasp. Osman's work has been engaged in a dialogue that seeks to make sense of a number of overlapping conversations, theories, politics, and broadly construed claims about blackness, queerness, Islam, and the post-colonial condition. The photographs below were produced in the context of engaging Frantz Fanon's essay on the veil, Fanon's claims to know nothing about homosexuality, and his importance as a post-colonial thinker; contemporary post-9/11 claims that the Muslim is a brown body even when African Muslims figure among detainees in Canada; and an attempt to complicate stories from all sides of the debate on queers, African, Muslims, Islam, and homosexual rights in the contemporary era.[13] The photographs cannot be consumed as terrorist pictures since these are not the usual images of Muslim men we get, and thus, in their refusal to be easily consumed, the photographs offer us a pedagogy of the unasked. Unasked because in our failure to ask questions, Black/African Muslim masculinities and sexualities become obscured and hegemonized in very particular ways as terrorist, patriarchal masculinities. The three photographs below ask something of viewers. They ask us to contend with that which we do not know. But the photographs also require us to know or at least imagine what we might know differently, and thereby the photographs force viewers into the arenas of ethics and maybe even morality. But for my purposes, I would say the photographs produce conditions for reimagining what we might already know.

These images point to the indecipherable and ask

that we make sense of blackness, queerness, and masculinity in both local and global terms where each leaks into the other seamlessly. But the images also require us as viewers to refuse contemporary "racialisms" of all sorts, especially narratives that disappear Black/African Muslims, queer Muslims, fem Black men, and so on. These are not queers in need of rescue by the West — for these are queers who even know how to find the cruising spots of the violent state and the playgrounds of pleasure for gay male sex (the park of Ontario's provincial legislature). Importantly, these photographs broaden the visual palette of Black masculinity's iconography.

I have taken the above long detour through Abu Ghraib to arrive at these photographs for many reasons. Chief among those reasons is the story of "Black masculinity" they tell. The varied palette of masculinities, the "femmed-out" Black maleness of a Black masculinity shrouded or veiled by religious and secular regimes and rhetorics of all kinds, refuses to cede any ground to our Black complicated and pleasurable Black queer selves. We must constantly struggle to claim our bodies. These images cast aspersions at lynching's history and Abu Ghraib's attempts to take our sex, sexuality, and ultimately our bodies away from us.

Used with permission of the artist — Abdi Osman
(from the Series *Discover Us* and *Queens at the Park*)

Life After Images

Most importantly, I think these photographs ask us to confront what I have come to call "critical diversity." Critical diversity does not only work at the level of representational inclusion; rather, critical diversity asks some difficult questions about inclusion and what inclusion signals and/or means in each context. Critical diversity is about both the texture and the depth of diversity. And by taking into account the texture and depth of diversity, its critical balance and calculation comes into play. Let me give an example of an ideal type of critical diversity. In the multicultural model, it might be sufficient to have some form of Black representation, maybe even multiple forms, but with critical diversity, those forms of multiple Black representation would have to account for a range of factors internal to blackness so that blackness is never homogenized. It might have to account for questions of class position, of disability, of sexuality, of religion, and so on in an attempt to get at the depth and the texture of how blackness is experienced and lived out in both its extra- and intra-Black differences. In short, it might have to account for the "Black Trans lesbian disabled body," a caricature that has come to be characterized in Black progressive vernacular political culture as an attempt to point to some of the ways in which Black bodies consistently disappear from our view. Imagine such a person! Thus, blackness in this instance cannot only be framed and understood in relationship to race and racism. Critical diversity seeks to not just populate our various arenas with one-dimensional encounters, it also seeks to provide encounters that strike deeply at the core of what it means to be human. Thus, critical diversity is about the ways in which categories or genres of the human cross-cut each other.[14] Critical diversity requires us to actively engage our imaginations and thus to imagine beyond the body presented to us.

I take it as an ethical given, then, that, fundamentally, only when some form of critical diversity is approached can we move towards social justice. Social justice is the greatest unknown in all this work. Social justice cannot be decided in advance, it has no particular destination, it is a process of coming into, a "to come" moment as Derrida would put it.[15] Social justice and indeed its achievement can only be known to be accomplished when those seeking it declare it to be so — that is, declare that social justice has been done. Thus, social justice is more a desire and a constant project to be worked on and worked at than a set of programs, a product, and/or a concluding deadline.

The post-1960s movements of civil rights, feminism, and gay and lesbian liberation produced moments through which movement towards social justice could be glimpsed, but those were merely moments in a process, an opening, if you will. Critical diversity provides other avenues along this process, but critical diversity is not the end point of social justice either, it is a part of it. What is most important and crucial about social justice and its philosophical and political call is that it opens us up to rethinking the entire process of any organization or, more broadly, formation, should it be necessary. Social justice, then, embeds critical diversity as a "normative" way of doing things, and thereby social justice is a way of being in the world. Social justice is a whole way of life, as Raymond Williams so famously named culture, it cannot be a type of training, and you can't run social justice workshops and trainings, despite the equity industry's claims.

Social justice is both an approach to living life and an orientation to thinking and imagining differently the present and the past as a way of setting in place the conditions for a different kind of future. It is that future my Black queer and Black Trans students have set out to write and create by living, studying, and acting out of the ordinary. Such a future tells the complicated and complex histories of Black masculinities as I have been attempting here.

Conclusion: In Defense of Black Canadian Boys; Redux

In contemporary North America, Black boys live queer lives regardless of sexuality. In the Canadian context, questions of Black masculinity cannot be divorced from the social and political institutions that govern belonging to the nation and citizenry. For example, in the Greater Toronto Area, figures suggest that 40% of Black children drop out of school. A majority of that 40% figure is Black boys and young Black men. Similarly, there is enough evidence to make the case that in the same region poor Black boys and young Black men are criminalized before they are even criminals. That process happens through over-policing of poor multiracial and multi-ethnic neighborhoods where it is common practice to request identification from youth, to record their home addresses, and so on under the guise of community policing. Thus, Black boys become Black men, particularly poor Black boys in the context of racism, poverty, health inequalities, the looming threat of unemployment, imprisonment, and death. Black masculinities are achieved, practiced, and lived out in the context of far-reaching political, social, and policy concerns. Nonetheless, it would be shortsighted to understand Black masculinities as only constituted through their victimization.

Despite the range of potential calumnies that can encircle the lives of Black boys and therefore young Black men, I hope that this essay demonstrates that Black boys and young Black men remain creatively and imaginatively engaged in their own world-makings and in the remaking and rethinking of the larger culture as Osman's photos point to. We live in a world where most often young Black men are not given credit for their creative and imaginative energies and contributions. The lack of such credit means that often when Black men act they do not always act in opposition or in creative reimagining of their masculinities but rather reproduce and produce the economy of stereotype in a range of practices as both a way to get by and many times as a mode of living a life, even a life that might be moving towards the very violences that both frame it and will end it. Black masculinities, then, remain complex, complicated, and ambivalent forms of human life where the historical and the contemporary continually meet to shape the present. What is particularly difficult about such meetings or intersections is that Black masculinities in such encounters almost always become singular. If we are to take the lives of Black men seriously, then we might want to dwell in the ambivalent space of living Black masculinity, a masculinity that I have elsewhere shown is both reviled and deeply desired.[16] In the immediate future, the question of poor Black masculinities lies somewhere between taking seriously the histories that Black boys carry as a part of the collective history of Black peoples; the histories Black boys carry as a part of the histories of men; and the histories Black boys carry as a part of the history of humankind.

First published in C. Greig and W. Martino (ed.). *Canadian Men and Masculinities: Historical and Contemporary Perspectives.* Canadian Scholars Press: Toronto, 2012, 191-204.

Notes:

1. Here, I am thinking of the work of R. W. Connell and other scholars of masculinity who have take his seminal insights as the basis for masculinity studies more generally

2. See the work of Sylvia Wynter, "1492: A New World View," for a discussion of how this dynamic arises in the colonial era and then comes to organize the last more than five hundred years of human life

3. "Paranoid Empire: Specters from Guantanamo to Abu Ghraib."

4. Judy, *(Dis) forming the American Canon*, 21

5. Ibid., 22

6. See also the work of Allan D. Austin *African Muslims in Antebellum America*

7. Eribon, *Insult and the Making of the Gay Self*, 15

8. Ibid.,17

9. Ibid., 16

10. Ibid., 79

11. Marriott, *On Black Men*, 9

12. Ibid.

13. See the work of Neville Hoad on Africa and Joseph Massad on the Middle East, who conceptually and historically tackle the questions of Africans, Arabs, homosexuality, and the ways in which contemporary conversations are always more complicated than merely one of rights and identity. In many ways, Osman's photography can be read as a visual element of this conversation

14. Here, I am thinking of Wilson Harris' notion of

cross-cultural resonance as always constitutive of who we are and Wynter's various articulations of the human as always already a hybrid form

15. See *Of Hospitality*

16. See Walcott "The Struggle for Happiness."

References

Austin, Allan. *African Muslims in Antebellum America*. New York: Routledge, 1997.

Derrida, Jacques. *Of Hospitality: Anne Dufourmantelle Invites Jacques Derrida to Respond*, translated by Rachel Bowlby. Stanford : Stanford University Press, 2000.

Ducat, Stephen. *The Wimp Factor: Gender Gaps, Holy Wars & the Politics of Anxious Masculinity*. Boston: Beacon Press, 2004.

Eribon, Didier. *Insult and the Making of the Gay Self*, translated by Michael Lucey. Durham : Duke University Press, 2004.

Harris, Wilson. "In the Name of Liberty." *Third Text*, Summer 1990: 7-15.

Hoad, Neville. *African Intimacies: Race, Homosexuality and Globalization*. Minneapolis : University of Minnesota Press, 2007.

Judy, Ronald. *(Dis)Forming the American Canon: African-Arabic Slave Narratives and the Vernacular*. Minneapolis: University of Minnesota Press, 1993.

Marriott, David. *On Black Men*. New York: Columbia University Press, 2000.

Massad, Joseph. *Desiring Arabs*. Chicago: The University of Chicago Press, 2007.

McClintock, Anne. "Paranoid Empire: Specters from Guantanamo and Abu Ghraib." *Small Axe*, No.28, Vol. 13, No. 1, March 2009.

Morrison, Toni. *Playing in the Dark: Whiteness and the Literary Imagination,* Cambridge: Harvard University Press, 1992.

Sharma, Parvez. (2007) *A Jihad for Love.*

Walcott, Rinaldo. "Reconstructing Black Manhood; Or the Drag of Black Masculinity." *Small Axe*, No. 28, Vol. 13, No. 1, March 2009.

——. "The Struggle for Happiness: Commodified Black Masculinities, Vernacular Culture, and Homoerotic Desires." *Pedagogies of Difference: Rethinking Education for Social Change*, edited by P. Trifonas. New York: RoutledgeFalmer, 2003.

Wynter, Sylvia. "1492: A New World View." In *Race, Discourse and the Origin of the Americas: A New World View*, edited by Vera Lawrence Hyatt and Rex Nettleford. Washington, DC: Smithsonian Institution Press, 1995.

61615340R00135

Made in the USA
Middletown, DE
12 January 2018